JIMMY CARTER
President and Peacemaker

JIMMY CARTER
President and Peacemaker

Nancy Whitelaw

**MORGAN
REYNOLDS**
Publishing, Inc.

620 South Elm Street, Suite 223
Greensboro, North Carolina   27406
http://www.morganreynolds.com

JIMMY CARTER: PRESIDENT AND PEACEMAKER

Copyright © 2004 by Nancy Whitelaw

Library of Congress Cataloging-in-Publication Data

Whitelaw, Nancy.
  Jimmy Carter : president and peacemaker / Nancy Whitelaw.— 1st ed.
      v. cm. — (Notable Americans)
Includes bibliographical references and index.
Contents: Back to Plains — Learning the ropes — Governor Carter —
Carter and Ford — Crisis of spirit — Campaigning again — From
President to world citizen — New opportunities — Promoting democracy
— Committed and tireless — We can choose.
  ISBN 1-931798-18-4
  1. Carter, Jimmy, 1924—Biography. 2. Presidents—United
States—Biography—Juvenile literature. [1. Carter, Jimmy, 1924- 2.
Presidents.] I. Title. II. Series.
  E873.W47 2003
  973.926'092—dc21

                              2003011662

Printed in the United States of America
First Edition

Notable Americans

Jimmy Carter

Ronald Reagan

Dolley Madison

Thomas Jefferson

John Adams

Andrew Jackson

Alexander Hamilton

George W. Bush

Lyndon Baines Johnson

Dwight D. Eisenhower

Ishi

Richard Nixon

Madeleine Albright

Lou Henry Hoover

Thurgood Marshall

Petticoat Spies

William Tecumseh Sherman

Mary Todd Lincoln

*To Betty Avery, with thanks
for all you have taught me about love.*

Contents

Jimmy Carter
(Courtesy of the Library of Congress.)

Chapter One

Back to Plains

When Jimmy Carter was six years old, he set his first goal. He wanted to join the navy and be a sailor like his Uncle Gordy who wore an impressive officer's uniform and sent postcards from exotic places where he served. "Exotic places" were anywhere far from the towns of Archery and Plains, Georgia, where Jimmy grew up. Jimmy was determined to gain admission to the Naval Academy in Annapolis, Maryland, just as his Uncle Gordy had. While still in elementary school, Jimmy began to study the entrance requirements to prepare for the Naval Academy.

Jimmy's home was much like those of his neighbors, without indoor water or electricity, and with a wood-burning cook stove. The family raised watermelons, cotton, corn, and peanuts. Most of the field work was done with a mule. Through hard work, commitments and responsibility, his father, James Earl Carter, achieved success as a farmer, businessman, and even served as a representative to the Georgia state legislature. Mr. Earl, as he was called, employed about two hundred share-croppers who worked on his farm and traded some of their crops for rent. He was exacting about finances. From his father, Jimmy learned to set goals and to commit himself to achieving them. Like other Southern fathers of his time, Mr. Earl sometimes punished his children by whipping them with a peach tree switch. Little Jimmy never forgot being whipped for taking a penny out of the church collection plate, and for shooting at his sister Gloria with his B.B. gun.

From his mother, known as Miss Lillian, Jimmy learned a commitment to public service and human rights. The only public health nurse in the area, Miss Lillian was ever ready with a bandage, a home-made

Jimmy Carter grew up in Plains, Georgia, in a home without electricity or indoor plumbing. *(Courtesy of the Jimmy Carter Library and Museum.)*

Carter's mother, Lillian, with six-month-old Jimmy in her lap. *(Courtesy of the Jimmy Carter Library.)*

remedy, and a dose of sympathy. Unlike Mr. Earl, Miss Lillian extended her compassion to blacks as well as whites. Miss Lillian said her Christian values led her to see the best in all people. She also encouraged a love of books. When she wanted one of the children to do a chore for her, she asked first what he was doing. If he said he was reading, she excused him from the task. Sometimes she invited family members to bring a book to the dining table, and they ate and read in silence.

James Earl Carter Sr., Jimmy's father, owned and ran a peanut farm in Plains, Georgia. *(Courtesy of the Jimmy Carter Library.)*

Growing up, Jimmy had plenty to do. He had two younger sisters and a little brother, a tree house, a tire swing, a pony, and bicycles. And there was always reading. Sometimes he worked in the fields, where one special chore was finding and killing boll-weevils on cotton plants. His relatives and neighborhood acquaintances remember Jimmy as a good boy. They also remember him as a determined young man who wanted to be the best, whether it involved baseball or high school debating or a Sunday school lesson.

While in high school, he did all he could to prepare for the Naval Academy admission exam. In his senior year, he worried his five-foot-three-inch height and one-hundred-twenty-one pound weight would keep him out. He gave up his part time job so he could rest more, on the theory that rest would make him grow. He also stuffed himself with bananas hoping they would fatten him up. He walked on Coca-Cola bottles to raise his arches so that he would not be turned down for flat feet, and he worried that his grades would not be good enough.

Like most of the whites in the area, the Carters accepted the segregationist policies of the times. The Carter children attended white schools in Plains and the all-white Plains Baptist Church. Jimmy later learned that black children were expected to lose at any game they played with whites. Racism was widespread, lynching was considered justified under certain conditions, and blacks were treated as inferiors from the time they were born. About half of the population of Plains attended black-only schools and churches, shopped at black-only stores, and ate at black-only restaurants.

From the time he was a young boy, Jimmy Carter prepared to attend the Naval Academy in Annapolis, Maryland. *(Courtesy of the Library of Congress.)*

In his last days of high school, Jimmy listened to radio broadcasts about the Japanese attack on Pearl Harbor, which led to America's entry into World War II. More than ever, he wanted to go to Annapolis so he could face his country's enemies as a military officer. His congressman did not grant him the required appointment to Annapolis in 1941, so he enrolled at Georgia Southwestern, a junior college. He did not get the appointment in 1942 either. He enrolled in Georgia Institute of Technology in Atlanta as a naval Reserve Officers Training Corps (ROTC) student to take courses in seamanship, navigation, and other military sciences recommended by the navy for students who wanted to get into Annapolis.

In 1943, Jimmy Carter received his eagerly awaited appointment to the Naval Academy. He had fulfilled a long-desired goal and felt a new confidence in himself. Most of his classmates were like him—white, middle-class Christians, and scholastic stars of their high school classes. Most knew about the traditional hazing they would have to endure at the academy—receiving paddlings with wooden spoons and breadboards, performing whatever humiliating tasks upperclassmen ordered them with a smile and a snappy "sir," and experiencing special harassment at meals. When Jimmy mentioned to an officer that he was going to attend a political rally, the officer told him to stay away from political meetings if he wanted a career in the navy. From that point on, Jimmy did not discuss politics. He accepted the navy's methods of training men without questioning, much as he had accepted his father's whippings without any show of weakness or fear.

The academy's regular four-year program had been condensed into three years since the war demanded more officers quickly. Jimmy's studies were mainly in engineering and mathematics, and he studied Spanish as his language elective. One of his classmates described him later: "Carter was very well liked by his company. But he was a loner . . . He didn't need other people's close bond of friendship." Following Jimmy's first year at the academy, in the summer of 1944, the Allied forces of Russia, France, Great Britain, the United States, and other countries landed in Normandy in a bold move against the Axis forces of Germany, Japan, Italy, and their allies. It was the beginning of the end for the Axis coalition.

In his last year at Annapolis, Carter focused on naval strategy, including navigation, gunnery, military law, ballistics, and thermodynamics. Learning was easy for him. His write-up in the year book said, "The only times he opened his books were when his classmates desired help on problems." He graduated 59 in a class of 820.

During his years at Annapolis, Jimmy met Rosalynn Smith, an alumna of Georgia Southwestern and a friend of Jimmy's little sister Ruth. Rosalynn was a pretty young woman and an excellent student. She was brought up with strict religious discipline that prohibited drinking and insisted on regular attendance at church, Sunday School, and Bible study.

Jimmy and Rosalynn were married on July 7, 1946.

Jimmy and Rosalynn married the summer after Carter's graduation from the Naval Academy. *(Courtesy of AP/World Wide Photos.)*

After a short honeymoon, Jimmy began his life as a navy officer in Norfolk, Virginia. The war was over, and Carter was assigned to teach high school level courses to enlisted men on the USS *Mississippi* in the Chesapeake Bay. He applied for a Rhodes Scholarship, a prestigious award, and was bitterly disappointed when he was rejected. He said later he felt he was the best candidate.

The Carter's first three children were boys: John William born in 1947, James Earl in 1950, and Donnel Jeffrey in 1952. Their marriage was typical of the times, in that the man was the head of the household and the woman did not consider a career outside the home. With

Jimmy away on duty much of the time, Rosalynn broke from her shyness and learned to assert herself.

Carter's career in the navy promised to be more exciting when, in 1948, he won a berth at a submarine school in New London, Connecticut. Submariners were chosen competitively, and Carter began to regain his faith in himself. He served as a junior officer on a conventionally powered sub. His fellow submariners remembered him as serious and hard working, more likely to be found reading than playing poker in his off-hours.

The Korean War, which began in June 1950, was originally a conflict between North and South Korea. It quickly spread, with involvement by nineteen other nations including the United States. It seemed that Carter's military career might take him into war. In

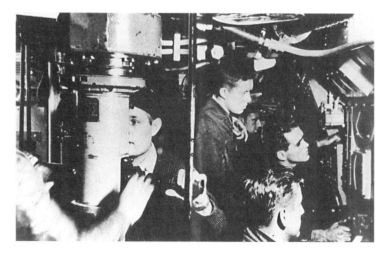

In 1948, Carter (*standing, rear*) was accepted as a junior officer in submarine school. *(Courtesy of the Library of Congress.)*

1952, by then a full lieutenant, he applied for work on a prototype atomic submarine, the USS *Sea Wolf*, under Admiral Hyman Rickover. In his first interview with Carter, the admiral asked about Carter's grade standing at Annapolis. Carter answered proudly that he had graduated in the top ten percent of his class. Rickover asked if he had done his best. Always honest, Carter admitted he had not always worked as hard as he might have. Rickover next asked, "Why not?" and Carter had no good answer. That question stayed in Carter's mind for the rest of his life. He was determined he would never again have to admit he might have tried harder.

He won the assignment with Rickover and found a hero in the admiral, a man Carter said always did his best and expected his sailors to do the same. A fiercely competitive, self-made man, Rickover was like Carter's father in that he accepted good performance without a word and criticized even the smallest mistake.

Carter was not called to fight in the Korean War, which ended in 1953. When his father died of cancer that same year, Carter was amazed at the hundreds of people who came to pay their last respects. It was only at his father's death that Carter learned how much his father had helped others. Mr. Earl had never mentioned that he paid off debts for people down on their luck, gave clothing to poor children, and helped widows. Carter resolved, "I want to be a man like my father." He believed he could better emulate his father on the farm than in the navy. Jimmy was determined to return to Plains, but Rosalynn was not. "I argued. I cried. I even screamed at him," she wrote in her autobiography. As a navy wife, she had found self-confidence and adventure, and she feared losing that by returning to Georgia. But it was more important to her that she not lose Jimmy, and in the summer of 1953, Rosalynn and Jimmy moved back to Plains.

The Carters returned to a near disaster on the peanut farm. The family business had sold about ninety thousand dollars worth of seeds for spring planting on credit. In an ordinary year, farmers would pay their bills after fall harvesting, but the summer of 1953 brought a drought that left farmers unable to pay their bills. Miss Lillian had paid no attention to her husband's business while he was alive, and when she heard of the financial crisis, she simply waited for Jimmy to come home to fix things.

In the first year that Carter ran the business, he netted less than two hundred dollars. He kept the debts on the books with the expectation they would be paid after the next harvest. A drought also occurred in 1954, and the list of unpaid debts doubled.

He now dedicated himself to making money with the same intensity that he had once dedicated to his studies at Annapolis. At the University of Georgia, he took courses in fence building, farm-record keeping, peanut and cotton growing, fish and pond management, and grain storage. He was fascinated with new machinery and farming techniques. He installed a modern peanut-shelling plant and expanded the business to sell nitrogen fertilizer as well as seed. Carter was determined to engineer a new hybrid peanut. Rosalynn matched his commitment to the business. After taking a course in accounting, she became a full-time partner, weighing produce, writing checks, and working with the book-keeping.

Both Carters enjoyed an extensive civic life with the Plains Baptist Church, a parent-teacher association, the local Lions Club, and a Boy Scout troop. Jimmy Carter began his political career as chairman of the county school board, president of the Plains Development Corporation, and president of the Crop Improvement Association.

Chapter Two

Learning the Ropes

In 1954 the United States Supreme Court ruled in a case called *Brown v. Board of Education of Topeka, Kansas* that segregated schools were unconstitutional. This set off a political firestorm throughout the South. The General Assembly of Georgia declared the decision null and void and threatened to close all public schools in the state if even one school tried to integrate. The Ku Klux Klan, a racist terrorist organization, reacted to the decision by throwing firebombs and setting fire to crosses on lawns of blacks. Businessmen in Plains organized a White Citizens' Council against integration. When Jimmy Carter refused to join the organization, his business was boycotted. For a short period, he lost about eighty percent of his business, but after some time, his customers came back to him.

There was little discernible integration in southwest Georgia until the 1960s, when the government attempted to enforce voting rights and integration of public facili-

Martin Luther King Jr. was a prominent leader of the civil rights movement in America until his assassination in 1968 at the age of thirty-nine. *(Courtesy of the Library of Congress.)*

ties. Two effective integration movements were the Albany Movement and the Student Nonviolent Coordinating Committee. They made a well-publicized Freedom Ride from Atlanta to Albany, the capital of the state. On one day, over a thousand people in an Albany Baptist church heard Dr. Martin Luther King Jr., who had emerged as a dynamic leader in the civil rights movement, speak on equality. He said his listeners would win if they just held out long enough. In the demonstrations that followed, several hundred men, women, and children were arrested, and Dr. King was sent to jail.

As the Albany Movement succeeded with a black voter registration drive, segregationists burned black churches and night riders shot into black homes where registration workers lived. For the most part, Carter stayed out of the racial turmoil in the 1950s and early 1960s.

In the fall of 1962, thirty-eight-year-old Carter announced his candidacy for the state senate. He ran in the Democratic primary and his campaign stressed his personal qualities as a family man, Annapolis graduate, businessman, and civic leader. When six thousand votes were counted, Carter had lost by 139. He discovered that Joe Hurst, a longtime Democratic political boss, had sat behind a registration table, told voters to scratch out Carter's name, and stuffed the ballot box with votes for Carter's opponent. Carter had a decision to make, and he had to make it fast. The general election would be held in less than three weeks. Should he shut his eyes to the fraud and work to get the Democratic Party behind him for his next run at election? Or should he expose the fraud and possibly lose any chance of running again as a Democrat in that area?

The decision was easy for Carter. He would not compromise the truth for political advantage. He confronted Hurst. "The law requires that people vote in secret and you're watching everyone," he said. He asked who was in charge. Hurst responded, "Doc [his friend] here is the poll manager and I'm the chairman of the Democratic committee, so I guess you could say we're in charge." Carter called in a reporter and told his story. The reporter answered, "Everybody knows it's not right, but this is the way we run elections here."

With about two and a half weeks to go before the general election, Carter asked for a recount. He prepared his case carefully, collecting statements from voters who had witnessed irregularities at the polling place. Five days before the general election, a recount committee ruled in Carter's favor. Unable to discover which ballots were tampered with, the committee threw out the entire vote from Quitman County. The presiding circuit court judge took both candidates' names off the ballot and called for a write-in election. Carter won by 831 votes. He became senator of the Fourteenth District of Georgia.

Carter had won more than the election. He had proven to himself and others he would be single-minded in his political goals. He had established himself as a person who could not be forced to play party politics. This was a new Carter. He had followed orders without question during his three years at the Naval Academy in Annapolis and after that in his seven years of active duty in the navy. As a businessman, he had learned to appreciate the freedom he had to make his own decisions.

During the forty-day Senate session, Carter became known as a hard worker, a senator who studied each issue diligently and played an active role in negotiations. He had earlier pledged to read every single one of the approximately one thousand bills that would come before him. Reading and studying came easily, but he would not rest on his laurels. He took a speed reading course to help him fulfill his pledge to read every bill. He was a member of a senate commission to improve education. He introduced a bill to increase state spending on education and to support an overall upgrading of Georgia's educational system. Yet he avoided the issue of racial segregation in schools.

In 1964, Carter won again in a race for the senate. He seized the opportunity to further his conservative fiscal policy. A tight budget was not new to Carter. His father's words, "always a reckoning," remained in his head. Soon after he had inherited his father's failing peanut business, he learned to tighten his belt and to improve business techniques. With this conservative fiscal experience, he introduced bills against the building of a six million dollar government building, against tax relief for senior citizens, and against a wage increase for state judges. He chaired committees that focused on promoting economic development.

His political successes spread his name and work beyond the boundaries of the area from which he was elected. He became a familiar figure on political platforms and in community meetings. He often wrote letters to editors, and he sent bulletins about his work and copies of his speeches to the people back home. In 1965, he was selected as one of the eleven most influential legislators in the state.

Supporters of Carter as a candidate for higher office advised him to avoid getting involved in the issues surrounding race. He ignored the advice when the Plains Baptist Church held a vote on whether to allow blacks to worship with them. He appeared at the church with Miss Lillian to cast his vote in the affirmative. When he learned the vote had gone against acceptance of blacks, Jimmy, his mother, and a few others started a new church nearby where blacks were welcome.

In May 1966, this relatively obscure state senator

from Plains announced his candidacy for governor of the state of Georgia. When they heard his announcement, many people asked, "Jimmy who?" This helped Carter emphasize his role of underdog and outsider, the perfect role for someone who was running on an anti-establishment ticket.

Carter conducted an extensive campaign of appearances and political meetings where he appealed to a popular following with his fiscal responsibility, his leanings toward the center of the political spectrum, and his record of honesty and integrity. He steadfastly refused to accept a label as either conservative or liberal. He said he was too complicated to be labeled.

He and Rosalynn set a goal of shaking 250,000 hands by the primary in September. On specific issues he stressed his commitment to economic development with support of improved public transportation and measures to decrease crime. On racial issues, he avoided questions as often as possible or vaguely referred to his position as moderate. He used the press well to portray himself as a family man with strong religious values, as well as a successful businessman. Rosalynn campaigned beside him much of the time.

In the final tally, he placed third in the primary. His spirits and his health were down. He was deep in debt. He had to watch Lester Maddox, a strident segregationist, take over as governor. Maddox won national attention when he stood at the door of his restaurant with an axe in his hand and declared, "There will be no integration here as long as I live."

Carter would later say that around that time he had been "born again." He reported his sister Ruth had "asked me if I would give up anything for Christ . . . I said I would." From that time on, he said, he experienced a deep inner peace through an intimate relationship with Christ. Bitterness about defeat would no longer be a part of his life. He said he learned to look at the future and ask himself how he could build on any setback. He read the Bible regularly and traveled to different states as an evangelist. On these trips, he and a partner knocked on doors of families suggested to them by the local preacher. At each house, they asked if the people were interested in accepting Christ as their savior. If the response was positive, they might spend the day praying with the potential converts.

It was following Carter's Christian reawakening that Rosalynn gave birth to their only daughter, Amy Lynn, in October of 1967. Now the father of four, Carter again turned to his political career. Re-reading the careful record he had kept of each religious visit, Carter saw a pattern. Gaining converts to Christ was similar to gaining supporters for a political leader. His mind turned to politics again, and he reviewed his unsuccessful attempt to become governor. Yes, he had lost decisively, but the campaign had brought him visibility and friends and had demonstrated his skill and charm as a campaigner. He had learned how to attack his opponents when necessary. Jimmy Carter was ready to return to the political scene, this time stronger, more determined, and more intense. One of his favorite philosophers,

Reinhold Niebuhr, had said, "The sad duty of politics is to establish justice in a sinful world." This marriage of politics and religion presented an exciting challenge for Carter.

He met with professional advisers Jody Powell and Hamilton Jordan to plan his second campaign for governor. They took polls and studied past elections for clues on issues to emphasize in his campaign. They started asking for donations right away, gathering the names of his friends and his business and church contacts into a list of potential donors. After each of his many speeches, he kept a record of names and addresses of people in the audience. His network rapidly grew in size and strength. The Democratic National Convention invited him to be a delegate. He refused the invitation, fearing he could be hurt by the intra-party strife over the controversial Vietnam War, in which American troops had been sent to South Vietnam to try to stop the spread of Communism. On this issue, he simply said he supported the way Republican President Richard Nixon was handling the situation.

Carter stepped up his personal appearances, shaking hands with people at factory lines, shopping centers, and football games. He greeted everyone with a smile and quick handshake, always looking people in the eye as he met them. He spent little time discussing issues. Later one of his aides was asked to explain how Carter became so popular so fast, and he answered, "How do you explain falling in love?"

In September of 1970, the polls showed Carter at

twenty-one percent of the vote and his chief primary opponent, former Governor Carl Sanders, at fifty-three percent. With the help of a few advisers who called themselves the Peanut Brigade, Carter conceived a plan to close that distance. He labeled Sanders as a liberal who refused to let Georgia Democrats have a voice in their party, and a governor who had ignored prison reform opportunities and provided inadequate financing for public schools. Carter appealed to segregationists by condemning bussing students to schools outside their neighborhoods as a way to integrate public schools. He also visited a private segregated school, and voiced support for George Wallace, the openly segregationist governor of Alabama. He believed he could gain an advantage with both black and poor white voters with statements such as: "What they [the voters] want is someone in the governor's office who understands their problems . . . what it means to be fearful of the system of justice, to have cold chills go up and down their spines when a patrolman stops 'em." He called his meticulously dressed opponent "Cufflinks Carl" and posed in jeans and plaid shirts as "Honest Farmer Jimmy."

As primary day approached, the margin between Carter and Sanders narrowed. When the votes were all counted, newspapers reported Carter had won a stunning political upset. Still, he failed to get a clear majority. In the run-off election, Carter beat Sanders. In the general election, he again won, this time with about sixty percent of the vote. The winner of the race for lieutenant governor was Lester Maddox, the segrega-

Jimmy Carter taking the oath of office as the governor of Georgia on January 12, 1971. *(Courtesy of AP/Wide World Photos.)*

tionist Democrat who had won over Carter in the 1966 gubernatorial election. Forbidden by law to be governor for more than one term, Maddox chose the second spot as his best chance to influence Georgia politics. Both men pledged mutual support after the election.

The inauguration ceremonies were elaborate, with an eight-by-four foot portrait of Carter woven from over two thousand camellias, a performance by the Naval Academy, and an all-black choir from Morris Brown College. A reporter described the family: "The 46-year-old Governor with his reddish hair and white toothy smile," and Rosalynn, "slim, and dark-haired in a trim green coat with a white fur beret, and their four children . . . looked young and beautiful and eminently photogenic."

Carter's most-quoted lines from his inauguration speech were: "The time for racial discrimination is over. No poor rural white or black person should ever have to bear the additional burden of being deprived of the opportunity of an education, a job, or simple justice." With these words, Carter turned his back on the racism he had grown up with, and seemed to embrace during the campaign, and declared his support for equality and justice.

Chapter Three

Governor Carter

The state Jimmy Carter now governed had been one of the poorest in the country until the mid-twentieth century. Then World War II brought Georgia an influx of military bases and the jobs that accompanied them. Citizens from rural areas and the inner cities did not benefit from this economic growth, however, and most of them remained in the cycle of poverty and unemployment that had been the lot of their families for generations. Conflict over integration dominated other state issues. The political system was riddled with fraud.

Carter manned his staff with people he knew would be loyal, and placed his friends in key leadership positions Georgia's Democratic Party. Hamilton Jordan became his executive secretary, and Jody Powell his press secretary. A small group of lawyers who had worked with Carter on his campaigns became his cabinet. Members of Carter's family were active in his administration. Rosalynn was particularly interested in mental health issues. Jack, at twenty-three the oldest Carter child, did some liaison work with the general assembly. Twenty-one-year-old Chip and eighteen-year-old Jeff worked in the governor's office.

Carter's daily schedule began each morning before 7:00 A.M., when he had a meeting with his secretaries. At 8:00 A.M., he scheduled meetings with visitors, granting ten or fifteen minutes to each. He set aside time each day for reading, studying issues, and responding to mail. He generally ate lunch while he worked and read. In the afternoon, he kept appointments, gave speeches, or continued studying. Every Thursday, he held a press conference. Once a month, for two hours in the afternoon, he held interviews with groups of his constituents at an event he called "Speak Up Day." On most days, he took home a briefcase of memos to work on after dinner. He frequently entertained friends and potential supporters with barbecues, dinner, and entertainment at the governor's mansion. Occasionally, he would give a speech or attend a charity event in the evening. Saturdays were usually reserved for putting in an appearance at a local event. On Sunday, the Carter family attended the Northside Drive Baptist Church, where Carter sometimes taught a Sunday School class. The governor's mansion was open to visitors on Sunday afternoons.

Carter initially addressed the need for fiscal reorganization by implementing the concept of zero-based budgeting. Under this process, each government department summarizes its goals and outlines a procedure for them. Top administrators give each report a priority, and funds are granted on this basis. Although the process sounded efficient at first, Carter soon realized there was no way he could personally review each of the eleven thousand reports. He also discovered that department heads would adjust their reports as they learned about the availability of funds. Carter soon learned to follow the example of his predecessors and review only those reports that requested a change in budgeting or were blatantly questionable.

Along with zero-based budgeting, Carter appointed a planning group to prepare a comprehensive plan for reorganizing the state government. The final plan was a compilation of studies and advice from legislators, lobbyists, business leaders from such companies as Sears and Delta Airlines, and university faculty members. Among the issues considered by the group were the consolidation of government hiring and firing policies, transferring certain responsibilities from one department to another, centralizing computer operations, and allowing the governor to impose a veto when he felt it necessary. Carter proved to be a shrewd politician in face-to-face meetings, able to talk potential opponents into supporting him. Although Maddox fought against the reorganization bill, Carter bragged he got ninety-five percent of what he had initially wanted.

With his background as school board president and work in the senate committee on education, Carter gave education a high priority in his administration. He was intent on equalizing educational opportunity and his themes were quality, equity, and accessibility. Under pressure from Carter, the Early Childhood Development Act committed Georgia to a statewide kindergarten program.

Under his reorganization, the Department of Natural Resources gave environmentalists both more money and more political clout. Enforcement procedures were strengthened. He also proposed measures to prevent erosion, regulate flood hazard areas, and provide checks against developers who might otherwise cause damage to the environment. Development along the Chattahoochee River led him to assert that when private exploitation threatened the environment, he would not hesitate to suggest public control. Originally he was in favor of a freeway which would connect Stone Mountain with downtown Atlanta, an idea conceived to relieve congested traffic flow. When the study commission he appointed reported that construction of such a freeway would destroy historic parks and residential housing, he withdrew his support.

The relationship between Carter and Maddox grew increasingly contentious. Early on, neither man would admit publicly to their problems, but as time passed, their rift became public. In one version of a meeting they had, Carter told Maddox that when Maddox opposed him he would fight with every bit of authority he had. Maddox answered he would fight back.

Once Carter spoke with a group that protested the Equal Rights Amendment (ERA), which called for equality of the sexes under law. The protestors quoted

St. Paul in the New Testament saying that wives should be subject to their husbands. The day after he had this meeting, Rosalynn appeared in his office waving a large red, white, and blue banner that said "ERA— YES." The next day, he spoke in favor of ERA legislation. When it was defeated, he said he was disappointed.

Often he repeated his campaign pledge to end racial discrimination. All departments in his administration were required to follow a policy of nondiscrimination in hiring and firing as well as in day-to-day operations. He ordered a portrait of Dr. Martin Luther King Jr. displayed in the state capitol, an honor reserved for whites until that time. For these and other such acts, he was awarded an honorary degree from predominantly black Morris Brown College of Atlanta. In racial conflicts, as well as in other issues, he was aware that granting a right to one group might negatively impact another's rights, as in school integration through mandatory bussing. He rejected quotas as the answer to discrimination in employment, education, and housing. He instead committed himself to working for the best possible opportunities for all.

Carter's term as governor would expire in 1975, and under the state constitution, he was not eligible for a second term. He was proud of his accomplishments as governor, and he wanted to continue to work in government. His commitment to public service was stronger than ever, as was his belief in his ability to lead. With input from his aides Hamilton Jordan, Jody Powell, and Peter Bourne, Carter decided he would make a run for president in 1976. Carter's campaigns so far had focused on his being an outsider. This role would continue to be appropriate for a national electorate disillusioned with the Vietnam War, poverty, rising unemployment, and an increasing distrust of government in general.

Carter and his advisors set up a strict schedule to prepare for the campaign, which included reading national newspapers every day, studying previous elections, and becoming current on matters of defense, foreign policy, and the economy. They set up task forces to advise Carter on different issues and to expand his Washington contacts. These advisors suggested he smile frequently to bring back memories of the beloved President John F. Kennedy who had been assassinated, as well as to capitalize on his strongest asset—personal charm. They agreed he should keep his plan to run for president secret until the campaign was fully organized. If he announced to early, there would be more time for opponents to criticize him.

In March 1973, Carter sought and won appointment as co-chairman of the national Committee to Elect Democrats. He spent hours meeting with leaders of groups that traditionally supported Democrats—labor unions, farmers, teachers, women, government workers, blacks, and environmentalists. He initiated meetings with wealthy potential donors to the party. He focused on issues important to poor and middle class people such as crime, drugs, tax reform, and governmental waste.

President Richard M. Nixon resigned as president of the United States in August of 1974. *(Courtesy of the Library of Congress.)*

Because of all his travels related to his presidential bid for 1976, Carter's popularity in Georgia slipped. To recover this support, he ordered new funding for roads, environmental projects, and recreation areas for blacks, including community swimming pools, a luxury long denied them. He encouraged citizens to attend meetings, to write letters, and to give suggestions about government. He quickly became known as a leader who would answer letters, often with a personal note. To citizens who seemed irrevocably opposed to his views, he wrote that they should register and vote against him.

In June 1972, a major scandal engulfed President Richard M. Nixon and many of his supporters. Five burglars were caught in the offices of the Democratic National Committee at the Watergate office complex in Washington, D.C. Their arrest eventually uncovered a White House sponsored plan of political espionage involving the president's attorney general, chief of staff, and other key advisors. Congressional investigators finally accused President Nixon himself of authorizing payments to the burglars. After two years of Congressional hearings and revelations made by investigative reporters, President Nixon resigned in August 1974. His resignation fueled Carter's hopes for a successful run for the presidency.

In December 1974, one month before his term as governor was up, Carter announced his candidacy for president. As evidence of his qualifications, he boasted of his reorganization of state government, including the consolidation of three hundred offices and commissions into twenty-two new agencies. He had instituted zero-based budgeting and opened government meetings to the public. The number of black state employees rose from just under five thousand to over 6,500 during his tenure. He reinstituted the death penalty and worked for stiffer sentences for drug violators. He had a strong record on environmental issues. Critics responded that Carter failed to mention government expenditures had risen sharply during his term, and his reorganization achievements looked better on paper than they did in reality.

Chapter Four

Carter and Ford

Carter started on the presidential campaign trail in January 1975, speaking with enthusiasm and confidence about his chances of winning. As in his earlier political races, calling himself an outsider was a big advantage. He emphasized he was not a part of Washington, where the Watergate scandal, the Vietnam War controversy, rising unemployment, and increasing poverty had led to distrust of national leaders. He chose as his campaign slogan, "For the American Third Century, Why Not The Best?" By June, he and his staff had traveled more than fifty thousand miles, visited thirty-seven states, and appeared on nearly one hundred radio and television shows.

He wrote everywhere he went—scrawling on yellow legal pads, composing longhand in hotels and airports, and typing on his portable typewriter on weekends. He compiled some of this material into his first book, *Why Not the Best?*, released by Broadman Press, a Southern Baptist publisher of inspirational literature.

By September, he was offered Secret Service protection, as well as federal funds toward his campaign. Pundits disagreed on whether Carter's philosophy was more conservative or liberal. A *New York Times* reporter noted that, except for Carter, the front-running candidates for the nomination were all senators: Henry Jackson of Washington, Birch Bayh of Indiana, and Hubert Humphrey of Minnesota. Carter hoped his executive experience as governor would give him an edge over he group of legislators.

In June 1976, Carter was nominated for president on the first ballot at the Democratic National Convention in New York, with over twenty-two hundred votes. The next day, he named Minnesota Senator Walter Mondale, a liberal and a Washington insider, as his vice-presidential candidate. In his acceptance speech, Carter spoke against special privilege and influence, called for a fairer tax system, and accused the current administration of secrecy and dishonesty. He criticized inefficient bureaucracy, too-large federal agencies and departments, high unemployment, inflation, and a growing national debt. At the end of the convention, Martin Luther King Sr., a prominent black clergyman, gave the benediction, ending with, "Surely the Lord sent Jimmy Carter to come on out and bring America back where she belongs." Then everyone joined hands and sang "We Shall Overcome," the song that had become the theme for racial integration.

Carter started the campaign with a large lead in the public opinion polls over his opponent, former Vice

Jimmy Carter campaigned against Gerald Ford in a race for the presidency in 1976. *(Courtesy of the Library of Congress.)*

President Gerald Ford, who had become president when Nixon resigned from office. Like Carter, Ford was personally popular, but he had two big liabilities. His administration was facing the worst economic slump since the 1930s, and many voters rejected him because he had pardoned Nixon of any crimes committed in covering up his campaign's participation in the Watergate break-in.

On the campaign trail, Carter said the most important duty of a president was to guarantee his country freedom from attack and blackmail, as well as to carry out a responsible foreign policy, implying the foreign policy that led to the Vietnam War was irresponsible. He promised he would never let American troops become involved in the internal affairs of another country. He promised he could institute all his proposed reforms without a single government worker losing his job and without sacrificing any of the nation's social programs. He declared he was personally opposed to abortion but did not support a constitutional amendment prohibiting them. On the inflammatory Vietnam issue, he proposed a pardon for the thousands of young men who left the country to avoid the draft.

Potential supporters asked how he would meet the energy crisis that arose in the early 1970s when international oil prices dramatically rose. This crisis brought to light the United States' dependence on foreign oil. Congress made some attempts to enforce energy conservation, but the idea of turning down heating thermostats in winter, raising air conditioning thermostats in summer, and walking instead of driving for short errands did not appeal to a populace accustomed to using all the energy it wanted. The situation was exacerbated in 1973 during the Arab-Israeli war when the Arab oil-producing countries cut back on production and limited their shipments to the United States. America lacked a comprehensive program to encourage fuel conservation, produce more fuel, and develop alternate forms of energy.

Critics saw some contradictions in Carter's statements. They said he claimed to favor the use of nuclear power to ease the energy crunch except when he was in New Hampshire, where citizens opposed the construction of a nuclear plant in their state. He proposed cutting the defense budget by billions, except when stumping in states such as Florida, with large military bases. He praised black minister Dr. Martin Luther King Jr.

when speaking to black audiences, but not to conservative white audiences. One of his campaign managers said no one could tell precisely where he was going, but people believed in him as a person. Polls indicated Carter's greatest weakness was his "fuzziness" on issues. Carter answered that he was not fuzzy, but was more thoughtful than the other candidates.

On matters of race, Carter emphasized his role in the forefront of the civil rights movement. He promised to appoint blacks to a task force to define racial issues and to name more blacks to administrative posts after he was elected. Throughout the campaign, black voters helped Carter.

His religious beliefs played an important part in his campaign. He frequently told people he was a very religious man, a "born again Christian" who believed in the literal interpretation of the Bible. This made a favorable impression on many voters. It was a well-known fact that he sometimes taught Sunday school in the Plains Baptist Church, as well as an adult Bible class. He talked about how religion could win the battle over racial discord. He said of his fellow church members, "We've got something that never changes—faith in God!" He took care not to impose his beliefs on others or to criticize the lifestyles of anyone who worked for him. Rosalynn often talked about her husband's religious orientation on the campaign trail. She repeated frequently, "We need your help, so that with your help and the help of our Lord Jesus Christ, Jimmy Carter can be a great president of these United States."

Martin Luther King Sr., gave the benediction at the 1976 Democratic Convention. *(Courtesy of the Library of Congress.)*

Some important Jewish leaders reacted negatively to Carter's religious pronouncements. In response, Carter distributed letters saying he was committed to the independence of the state of Israel, and he worshiped the same God that Jews worshiped.

Carter exuded self-confidence and told people he did not want to be arrogant but he was sure of himself. He admitted he was stubborn and explained, "I don't know how to compromise on any principle I believe is right." He was a hard worker who often started his campaigning days at 5:00 in the morning and continued throughout the day. He read three or four books every week, including material about foreign affairs, history, the presidency, and campaign platforms—particularly those of unsuccessful candidates for president.

He insisted he never claimed to be better or wiser than any other person, and that his greatest strength was that he was an ordinary man. He carried his own luggage, washed his own socks, made his own bed, and relaxed in work shirts and blue jeans. He said, "If I ever tell a lie, I want you to come and take me out of the White House." Even those who did not support Carter admitted he had charisma. He somehow established an aura of intimacy, no matter how large the group to which he was speaking. Carter promised people they could trust him, and trust was just what millions of voters were looking for. As the summer moved on, Carter seemed more and more likely to be the winner in the fall election.

In September, Carter attracted unwelcome attention with his comments during a *Playboy* magazine interview. He said that, although he had never committed adultery, he had looked at women with lust in his heart. According to his religion, this was a sin. Also in that interview he used slang like "screw" and "shacks up." Immediately, newspaper headlines picked up his comments. The question arose: Was Carter the moral and religious person he professed to be? Ford said about Carter, "He wavers, he wanders, he wiggles, and he waffles."

The first Carter-Ford debate on national television had one hundred million viewers. Carter appeared tired and drawn compared to Ford's presidential demeanor. Reporters declared the debate a draw. In the second Carter-Ford debate, Carter was confident and aggressive, as was Ford. However, Ford made a mistake on a question about the Soviet sphere in Eastern Europe. The

Carter chose Minnesota Senator Walter Mondale as his vice-presidential candidate. *(Courtesy of AP/World Wide Photos.)*

reporter picked up on his mistake, and so did Carter when it was his turn to respond. With that mistake, Ford lost the debate by seventeen points to Carter's sixty-two. In the third debate, just two weeks before the election, Carter softened his attack on Ford. He pledged to stick to issues and said he would not make any more personal attacks. Neither man came out a clear winner in the polls taken after this final debate.

Just before the election, one national reporter declared the two candidates were just one percentage point apart because the people saw them as very much alike. There were twice as many Democrats as Republicans in the country, but historically Democratic turnout was lower than Republican. Pundits predicted the outcome would hinge on the weather. They said a sunny day would turn out more voters and thus result in a Carter victory. A dreary day would bring out only those voters who were doubtful of Carter and might prefer Ford because he was a known quantity.

On a sunny November 2, Carter won the presidency. In the electoral college he won by a vote of 297 to 240. In the popular vote of about eighty million cast, he won by a margin of less than two million. In Congressional elections, both houses held a Democratic majority.

Right from the beginning, Carter used symbols and speech of the "common man" in his presidency. For the swearing-in ceremony in front of the capitol, he wore an ordinary three-piece business suit. He used his campaign name, Jimmy Carter, instead of his given name, James Earl Carter Jr. His inaugural speech, shorter than most, concluded, "In a spirit of individual sacrifice for the common good, we must simply do our best." Then he broke all precedents by walking the mile and a half down Pennsylvania Avenue to the White House with Rosalynn and nine-year-old Amy beside him.

The new president followed through on his promise to create a simpler and less expensive presidency. Fewer flowers were bought for White House decoration. The Marine Corps Band did not play "Hail to the Chief" every time he entered a room. Chauffeur service for his aides was restricted. He insisted government regulations be written in plain and simple language, accessible to all. Five to ten percent of the guests at state dinners were "average" Americans.

President Carter was determined to enact measures to ensure that the hiring and firing of government workers would be decided solely on merit. Some legislators

Instead of riding in a limousine during his inaugural parade, Jimmy Carter broke with tradition by walking down Pennsylvania Avenue to the White House. *(Courtesy of UPI/Bettman Newsphotos.)*

complained Carter made appointments without consulting them, robbing them of the opportunity to reward campaign workers and donors. They also complained that projects of special interest to them were deleted from the budget without consultation. Carter insisted he would do what was right for the American people regardless of what was politically expedient.

During the campaign, Carter had promised an omnibus energy bill that would include both short- and long-term planning. He set the scene with a televised "fireside chat" beside a fireplace. He modeled energy conservation by wearing a sweater to remind citizens that rooms should not be extravagantly heated. His omnibus bill was not the simple piece of legislation he had promised. It was instead a mixture of many measures, such as phased deregulation of the price of new oil, an increase in natural gas prices, a tax on "gas guzzler" vehicles which consumed large amounts of fuel, and a tax deduction for homeowners who undertook energy saving efforts. Some of these measures ran counter to promises made by legislators to their constituents. Citizens were impressed by Carter's intentions, but did not follow through on his suggestions as he had hoped they would.

In his inaugural address, Carter had pledged to work toward a goal of eliminating nuclear weapons from the face of the earth. To accomplish this, he would have to reach an agreement with Soviet leaders. In 1972, the United States and the Soviet Union had signed an interim agreement known as Strategic Arms Limitation I (SALT I), which laid the framework for mutual limits on nuclear weapons and anticipated a SALT II agreement. Carter had every intention of following through on these talks and of pressing for détente, an easing of tension between nations. Carter's criticism of Soviet violations of human rights, though, understandably increased the tension. SALT II representatives met but achieved little. Perhaps in reaction to this stalling of progress, Carter softened his stance on Soviet violations, but he did not desist.

Chapter Five

Crisis of Spirit

In the meantime, worldwide terrorism was on the rise. In Washington, twelve religious extremists invaded three buildings and terrorized 134 hostages for thirty-nine hours before the hostages were released and the gunmen arrested. In the Netherlands, Indonesian terrorists held 166 children and adults for twenty days before an attack freed the captives. Palestinian and German terrorists kept more than eighty hostages on a hijacked jetliner until the plane was stormed by commandos. In Iran, militants, led by religious leader Ayatollah Ruhollah Khomeini, tried to topple the repressive Shah Mohammed Reza Pahlevi.

Carter's attention was focused on Panama, where anti-American protests had been increasing for decades. In 1903, the United States signed a treaty with Panama, which gave the U.S. permission to build and manage a canal that would link Panama's east and west coasts. Through the years, Panamanians put increasing pressure on the Untied States to release their control over the canal. Anti-American riots in Panama in 1964 were the impetus for a series of new treaties, none of which fully satisfied either the Americans or the Panamanians. Carter believed the best way to solve the conflict was to lobby for a new Panama Canal treaty that would grant full authority of the canal to Panama. Although this was not popular with Americans, Carter insisted: "We needed to correct an injustice. Our failure to take action after years of promises under five previous Presidents had created something of a diplomatic cancer." In April, the treaty was passed despite opposition from Congress and the citizens at large.

An Arab-Israeli conflict had dominated the Middle East since the 1967 Six Day War, in which Israeli forces wiped out Egypt's air force and land army. American efforts to bring about peace had so far been unsuccessful, but Carter, with his usual optimism, decided a face-to-face meeting of the leaders might bring them together to work for peace. He studied the issues. Israelis feared attack from the Arabs, and the Arabs feared domination by the Israelis. President Anwar Sadat of Egypt wanted Israel to guarantee eventual autonomy for residents of the West Bank and Gaza Strip. Israeli President Menachem Begin wanted limited home rule in those areas, with a review of the arrangement after three to five years. Sadat and Begin were hostile to each other personally as well as politically.

Begin had a reputation as an underground fighter and a radical right-wing politician, not a man anyone would have predicted to achieve peace with an Arab neighbor. Many in Washington believed Carter should let Begin know at the very first meeting what was acceptable to the United States and what was not. Carter chose instead to focus on Begin's desire for acceptance as the legitimate political leader of Israel.

Sadat had plotted against the Egyptian monarchy when it was dominated by Britain in the 1940s, was jailed for contacts with Germans during World War II, and took part in a successful coup against the Egyptian government in 1952. Carter knew that Sadat, like Begin, needed and wanted the respect of the international community.

Carter's aides wrote briefing papers for him. He complained, "You've got it all wrong . . . the fact is that they [Sadat and Begin] don't trust one another . . . I think I

The Ayatollah Ruhollah Khomeini overthrew the shah of Iran and seized power there in 1978. *(UPI/Bettman Newsphotos.)*

can bring them to understand each other's positions better." This thinking was basic to Carter's concept of conflict resolution, a concept that demanded mutual trust from both parties. All three men knew Begin and Sadat could not get along on a personal level and had little or no foundation on which to build mutual political agreements. Still, in September 1978, Begin and Sadat met with Carter at Camp David, the presidential retreat in Maryland.

Carter explained the procedure known as conflict resolution where a neutral mediator helps parties work out their own solution to a conflict. The first time he tried to get them to talk together, a shouting match ensued. After the second day of vain attempts to get the two men talking to each other, Carter gave up on meetings. Instead, he conducted shuttle diplomacy, going first to one man and then the other, looking for points of agreement. All communication between the two men was accomplished in this way.

Carter conceived an ingenious innovation to the problem of personal conflict between Begin and Sadat. He asked each leader to appoint a member to a drafting committee to work toward a solution. These two men met with Secretary of State Cyrus Vance and Carter. Freed from the hostility that had marked the meetings of Begin and Sadat, the members of this committee found mutually acceptable solutions to some of the problems. The fact that Sadat and Begin heard of these solutions from their own appointees made the ideas much more palatable than if the opposition had broached them directly. Carter kept the press away from the meetings, assuring that the parties could speak frankly without fear of being misinterpreted or misquoted.

In these meetings, Carter showed two sides of himself. He was the optimistic Christian who believed there was good in everyone, and he was the determined leader who used heavy-handed influence to ensure the talks continued. On the tenth day, when Sadat hinted he wanted to go home, Carter literally blocked the door and insisted he listen while the president told him a failure at Camp David would seriously damage Carter's reputation both at home and abroad. Sadat agreed to stay.

When the summit ended on September 17, after twelve days of negotiations, the Egyptian and Israeli leaders had agreed on a framework for peace between Egypt and Israel, and a framework for peace in the Middle East. They agreed on the withdrawal of Israeli forces from Egyptian territory and the normalization of relations between the two countries. In another agreement, vague promises were made regarding the land on the West Bank and Gaza. These accords were Carter's greatest diplomatic triumph as president. His popularity in the polls rose from thirty-eight percent in June to fifty-six percent in the fall.

This popularity did not last long, however. The administration's program of wage and price standards was unpopular. When corporate profits soared by as much as twenty-five percent, labor leaders demanded wage hikes higher than those proposed in administration guidelines. A tight budget required cuts in health, education, urban aid, and jobs. Carter's brother, Billy, who had a reputation for irresponsible comments and behavior, made anti-Semitic remarks in Libya, which damaged Carter's relationship with Jewish constituents. The Organization of Petroleum Exporting Countries (OPEC) placed embargoes on sales to the United States. Shortages of gas resulted in long lines at gas stations. Congress slashed funding for Carter's wage insurance plan, defeated his proposal for standby gasoline rationing, and voted to reinstate controls on oil. Carter's long-time friend and advisor Bert Lance was forced to resign because of financial deals he was involved in before coming to Washington to serve as director of the Office of Management and Budget. After Lance resigned, reporters began asking questions about Carter's promises to bring honesty to government.

Carter conceived a long-term solution to the energy problem. The solution included a limit on imported oil, gradual price decontrol of domestically produced oil, a stringent program of conservation, and development of alternative sources of energy such as solar, nuclear, and geothermal. He decided to explain his plan on television.

Just twenty-four hours before he was scheduled to appear on television, Carter told his advisors he had to cancel the speech. Last-minute hunches convinced him the speech would flop, and he feared he would be worse off than before. Advisors told him he would lose all

Jimmy Carter with Egyptian President Anwar Sadat (left) and Israeli Prime Minister Menachem Begin (right) at the signing of the Camp David Peace Accords between Egypt and Israel. (*Courtesy of the Jimmy Carter Library and Museum.*)

credibility with the American people if he canceled, but Carter was determined he would not speak until he had more input from government advisors and representatives from business. Cancellation of the talk led to rumors about why Carter did not face the American people as scheduled.

In typical Carter style, the president requested face-to-face meetings with dozens of advisors and over one hundred people from the media, businesses, unions, and civil rights organizations. He invited them to come to Camp David to confer and brainstorm with him. They came, and Carter listened to their criticism of his failures to solve energy problems, to keep inflation down and to work with Congress. He heard doubts about his ability to handle these and other existing problems. Many admitted they had supported him because he had been an outsider, but now, they said, they realized a president needed to be an insider to work with domestic and international problems. Carter wrote later, "It was not pleasant for me to hear this, but I felt their analysis was sound." One reporter summarized Carter's handling of the meetings: "It is a highly personal anti-institutional method, and it combines in some odd proportions humbleness and notions almost of royalty. Carter is . . . the majestic leader who goes freely and willingly among his people."

After the meetings, Carter made a television presentation he knew would make or break his presidency. He admitted he had made mistakes, and he spoke of the lack of trust between citizens and the government. He referred to a "crisis of spirit . . . All the legislation in the world can't fix what's wrong with America. What is lacking is confidence and a sense of community." The speech was well received. He made some staff changes that also gained support. But the energy crisis continued, environmentalist groups opposed his proposed organization of a powerful Energy Board, inflation and unemployment rose, and urban communities did not find the economic relief they had requested.

In early September, sixty-two percent of Democrats said they preferred Massachusetts Senator Edward

Kennedy to Carter as the next presidential nominee. A bandwagon for Kennedy grew with endorsements of several important labor union leaders, the National Organization of Women, and the National Conference of Democratic Mayors.

Carter responded with a well-financed program to reach voters personally in a bid for re-election. Rosalynn, their son Chip, Vice President Mondale and Carter telephoned voters every night. Every two weeks Carter met with editors and journalists. Rosalynn campaigned almost full time for her husband. In one spectacular week, Mondale campaigned in eleven cities in five days.

Carter could not have predicted the major blow that would come to his campaign from the Middle East. In Iran, Shah Mohammed Reza Pahlevi faced an unemployment rate of thirty-five percent, stagnant industrial production, and a currency that had lost fifty percent of its value. When citizens protested, he sent his secret police to threaten, torture, and kill dissidents. This move increased the strength of the dissidents, and a revolutionary movement grew more insistent.

This movement affected the eight hundred American soldiers stationed in Iran for tasks ranging from flight instruction to maintenance of sophisticated equipment. Iran could no longer guarantee their security. One night an American officer called Washington to report he was lying on the floor of his unheated house with the shades drawn. Two hundred Iranians were outside shouting, "Death to the Americans!" One officer was shot from

While Carter was president, militant students in Iran held fifty-two American citizens hostage for 444 days. *(Courtesy of AP/World Wide Photos)*

behind while unlocking his front door. Military personnel and dependents were hastily evacuated and returned to the United States as revolutionaries forced the shah to leave the country.

The shah was replaced by seventy-nine-year-old Ayatollah Khomeini. Khomeini was supported by the Palestinian Liberation Organization (PLO)—a political body organized to create a nation for Palestinians and to destroy Israel—and by the Soviet Union. Khomeini appointed vigilantes who were empowered to search out enemies of the government. He set up a system of courts that sentenced four to five hundred dissidents to execution during the first seven months of his rule. Khomeini declared all problems in Iran—poor transportation, lack of food, slow oil production—the fault of the United States or other foreign powers. The American embassy in Tehran remained open, even though revolutionaries stormed the building in February. In May, one hundred thousand demonstrators broke into the compound and tore down the flag. Carter recommended that Americans in Iran leave the country.

Initially, Carter had refused to listen to the exiled shah's pleas to be allowed to come to the United States for cancer surgery. He feared the reactions from Iranians who wanted the shah to return to Iran for sentencing and punishment, and from Americans who saw no reason to help the former ruler who had treated his citizens inhumanely. Eventually, however, Carter decided to allow the shah to come to the United States for medical help. In October, Carter granted permission for the visit.

Protesting this kindness to the shah, a group of militant students seized the U.S. Embassy in Tehran, and bound and blindfolded the staff. The sixty-three Americans were to be held hostage until the Americans agreed to send the shah back to Iran to stand trial for his crimes. Carter refused to extradite the shah. He called a halt to U.S. oil imports from Iran and froze Iranian assets in the United States. He considered breaking off diplomatic contacts with Iran but held out for the possibility of face-to-face negotiations with Iranian hostage-takers or government officials.

Chapter Six

Campaigning Again

The hostage situation in Iran was just one of many crises the American government faced in the fall and winter of 1979. Oil prices skyrocketed, interest rates rose to twenty percent, and inflation soared. In Afghanistan, communist supported rebels seized power. This pushed Islamic traditionalists to stage their own revolt. On December 28, Russian tanks and troops moved into Afghanistan to support the communist government. President Carter declared the Soviet act a grave threat to peace. He announced an embargo of economic and cultural exchange with the U.S.S.R, including a boycott of the 1980 Olympic Games in Moscow, if Soviet troops were not out of Afghanistan by mid-February. Carter announced his "Carter Doctrine" that declared any threat to the Persian Gulf region would be regarded as an assault on the vital interests of the United States. With this statement of foreign policy, Carter became the first president since Woodrow Wilson to try to reform repressive regimes in other nations.

In the middle of December 1979, a hope for the American hostages arose as the International Court of Justice at The Hague unanimously called on the Iranians to release them. If they did not, United Nations Secretary General Kurt Waldheim would fly to Tehran to negotiate their release. There was no immediate movement by the hostage takers in response to this demand.

In a return to Russian problems, Carter criticized the Soviet Union for trying to silence Dr. Andrei D. Sakharov, a Soviet nuclear physicist and political dissident. Carter supported Sakharov, saying "Human rights is the central concern of my administration." In further support of human rights he proposed spending forty-five million dollars for transmitters to broadcast Radio Free Europe and Radio Liberty more widely over Europe and Asia. He declared: "Tapping this new spirit [a demand for basic human rights] there can be no nobler nor more ambitious task for America to undertake in this day . . . than to help shape a just and peaceful world that is truly humane."

By Christmas 1979, the hostages had been held for six weeks. The annual festivities surrounding the lighting of the huge Christmas tree on the White House lawn were canceled because of the Iranian situation. Carter and his family believed that there was no place for a joyous Christmas celebration while the hostages were held captive.

Two days after Christmas, the Soviets launched a deployment of about nine thousand troops into Afghanistan, saying they had been asked by the Afghani leaders to quell the rebels. Carter said this was direct aggression on the part of the Soviets and a prelude to Soviet take-overs in Pakistan and the rich oil fields of the Persian Gulf. He wrote in his diary, "This is the most serious international development that has occurred since I have been President." He resolved "to lead the world in making it [the act of aggression] as costly as possible." He would use economic measures to force the Soviet Union to withdraw, "interrupting grain sales, high technology, fishing rights, reexamining our commerce guidelines . . . asking Australia and Canada not to replace the grain we might withhold."

Before the Soviet response was given, Carter received word the hostages were being denied basic rights. They were confined in a semi-darkened room, had their hands tied day and night, and were not permitted to speak to fellow hostages. Through the United Nations, the administration engaged in secret behind-the-scenes contacts with the Iranian administration. Slowly, the diplomats were fashioning an arrangement under which the hostages would be freed and the Iranian government would save face by announcing they were acting in the best interests of their country. Suddenly and without warning, Khomeini announced in March that he would not allow the release of the hostages to the United States. All further attempts to mediate with the Iranians were futile.

In a surprise move in April, Carter sent six C-130 transport planes, eight helicopters, and a team of commandos to rescue the hostages in Iran. When one of the helicopters struck a transport plane, eight American servicemen died, and four others were badly burned. The rest of the rescue team escaped, but they were not able to free the hostages. Iranian militants put the charred bodies of the eight servicemen on display in the still occupied United States Embassy. Many reports of the incident concluded that Carter had tarnished the honor of the country and had lost control of his administration with this failed attempt at rescue.

Carter had said earlier that he could not campaign for re-election when there were so many issues demanding his attention internationally. A reporter at a press conference noted that the election was only a few months away and asked when Carter was going to make public appearances again. He answered he would do so immediately, he could do nothing for the hostages right away. He said sanctions against the Soviet Union had been defined, Congress was looking favorably at his anti-inflation proposals, and it seemed the country would soon have a comprehensive energy policy. "None of these challenges are completely overcome, but I believe they are manageable enough for me to leave the White House on a limited travel schedule," he said.

A straw poll taken in July 1980 showed only twenty-three percent of the Democrats had high confidence in Carter's ability to lead the country. Senator Kennedy announced his candidacy for president and was immediately hit with questions about scandals in his private life.

In August, Carter received the Democratic nomination to run again, beating Kennedy 2,129 to 1,146. The nomination was his, but the party was divided and had a low standing in the polls. The Republican nominee, California Governor Ronald Reagan, was already ahead. Reagan appealed to voters with his often asked question, "Are you better off now than you were four years ago?"

Reagan supporters hammered Carter with criticism. They said he had not restored fiscal balance to the country. They asserted that United States relationships with the Soviet Union, Iran, Afghanistan, NATO allies, and Israel were in disarray. The Camp David peace progress had stagnated. Carter was not working well with Congress. His domestic energy program was twisted beyond his original intention.

Carter supporters declared that events beyond Carter's control, such as the energy crisis, were responsible for the economic problems of the country and for problems with international relations. They asked voters to understand that Congress had as much responsibility as the president to maintain a balance between the executive and the legislative branches of the government. Supporters of Carter praised his commitment to peace and justice, his readiness to talk face-to-face with those who opposed him, his intelligence and study of all issues, and his mediation techniques. They said he embodied the qualities citizens asked for most often in their leaders: integrity, honesty, and commitment.

On election day, only about fifty-two percent of eligible voters went to the polls. At 9:01 P.M. on November

4, 1980, before the polls had closed in California, Carter called Governor Reagan to congratulate him on his victory. At headquarters, he wept, "I can't stand here tonight, and say it doesn't hurt." Reagan won the election by fifty-one percent to Carter's forty-one percent.

In his last months in office, Carter conducted an intensive campaign to maneuver through Congress bills he suspected a Republican administration would stall or ignore. These bills supported environmental causes such as protection of wetlands and desert ecosystems, funding for alternative energy sources such as natural gas and solar power, and legislation which mandated cleaning up toxic waste dumping grounds. He saw the Alaska Lands Act signed into law, an act that almost tripled the area of United States land designated as wilderness. He vetoed a bill that would have prohibited the Justice Department from intervening in lawsuits

Jimmy Carter lost his bid for reelection in 1980 to former movie star and governor of California Ronald Reagan. *(Courtesy of the Ronald Reagan Presidential Library.)*

over bussing to achieve school integration. He established a grain reserve to help alleviate world hunger, and he set aside funds for research into the use of methane gas as a practical automobile fuel.

Just before Christmas 1980, more than a year after their capture, the Iranian government demanded the United States pay twenty-four billion dollars to ransom the hostages. Carter refused. On January 6, fourteen days before the presidential inauguration, the Iranians lowered their ransom demand to twenty billion dollars. Further negotiations brought concessions from the administration: writing off Iran's debts to the United States, freeing of Iranian assets frozen by the administration, and an end to the trade embargo against Iran.

On Inauguration Day, January 20, the hostages were released moments after Ronald Reagan was sworn in as president. Still today, many insist the release was the result of a secret agreement between Reagan and Iran. These rumors were reinforced later when Republican senators blocked the financing of an investigation into the release. Another theory about the release was that the Iranians feared that Reagan's handling of the situation would be less patient and more hostile than Carter's.

At President Reagan's request, Carter agreed to travel from Plains, Georgia, to Wiesbaden, Germany, to greet the returning hostages. Although the failed rescue mission haunted him then and for the rest of his life, Carter said meeting the hostages face-to-face was one of the most satisfying things he had ever done. When he returned to Plains, Carter was totally exhausted. After sleeping for twenty-four hours, he announced that he saw ahead of him "an altogether new, unwanted, and potentially empty life."

Carter was frustrated but not broken. From the time he was six years old and resolved to join the navy, he had set and met goals for his private, political, and business life. There was no established role for an ex-president. Typically, ex-presidents wrote their memoirs, established presidential libraries and traveled a speaking circuit. Carter had attained international credibility through his accomplishments at Camp David, the Panama Canal treaties, and his human rights advocacy. Now he resolved to make the most of this credibility in a renewed determination to help bring peace and justice to the world.

Before he could attend to the larger problems of the world, he had to deal with the million dollar debt the family peanut business had acquired under the management of his brother Billy. Carter's retirement pay was less than seventy thousand dollars a year, so, both grieving and embarrassed, he sold the business to relieve some of the debt.

There was still more debt to be paid. The quickest way for Carter to raise more money was to write a memoir. His attention to detail and careful note-taking during his presidency paid off. He had faithfully kept diaries that filled six thousand double-spaced pages, written thousands of notes, messages, and reports, and tape-recorded lengthy entries. His agents negotiated a multimillion dollar deal for him. He insisted on two restrictions. One was that he would not spend more than a year on the book. The other was, "I'm not going to try to write an apology or rationalization of what we did." Rosalynn also wrote a memoir. They joked about whether Rosalynn's *First Lady from Plains* or Jimmy's *Keeping Faith* would be more popular. Both were on the *New York Times* best-seller list.

For just a few months after his presidency had ended, Carter stayed out of politics. He privately fumed about Reagan's close ties with South Africa's white minority government, the permission he granted to sell oil and gas leases off the coast of California, and his support of countries like Argentina, Paraguay, and Uruguay despite their flagrant violations of human rights. Then in July, Carter gave a press conference in which he said Reagan's budget cuts threatened the poor, the sick, and the unemployed, and that sales of weapons abroad could lead only to open conflict. The speech sent a signal that Carter would no longer be quiet about politics.

Chapter Seven

From President to World Citizen

Carter soon acted on his determination to help bring peace and justice to the world. He announced the creation of the Carter Center, a place to solve disputes, both nationally and internationally, with conflict resolution methods. For the next few years he spent many hours refining his goals for the Center and seeking funds from grant-giving boards and foundations.

With firm plans drawn up for the Center, Jimmy and Rosalynn began a schedule of international visits unequaled by any president, either sitting or retired. On their visit to China, the couple pushed a human rights agenda by asking President Deng Xiaoping to review the cases of Chinese political dissidents. The Carters went on to Japan where Carter was greeted with honor as a global statesman. There he asked for and received $2.5 million for the Carter Center. In September 1982, Carter accepted a teaching position at Emory University, a private coeducational institution in Atlanta. Most of the next year was filled with teaching schedules and continuing plans for the Carter Library.

When he was invited to Cairo as a guest of the Egyptian government, Carter plunged right back into political conflict. During an interview before he went, he announced he might meet with Yasir Arafat on that trip. Both the Reagan administration and the Israeli government reacted quickly, asking Carter not to speak to Arafat. He gave in reluctantly but said he might meet with other representatives of the PLO. During that trip, which he said he made as an Emory University professor, not as a United States representative, he met with Egyptian President Hosni Mubarak and talked with as many local officials and other Egyptians as he could. As president, Carter had established a firm reputation as a man determined to bring peace and justice to all. As ex-president, this reputation, plus his friendly and open manner and genuine interest in both people and events, brought him a warm welcome everywhere, especially in those areas of the world where the United States administration displayed a more critical attitude.

At an ancient Coptic Orthodox Church in an Egyptian village, he was asked to intervene with Mubarak to secure the release of a priest who was being held as a political prisoner. It took Carter twenty-one months of persistence, but he finally achieved the release. By accepting this plea, Carter showed the world that issues of human rights would always be an important concern for him. Some said the former president had become a missionary.

In Israel, Carter and Begin went on a tour of the West Bank and Gaza. Teenage Palestinians threw bottles at them and shouted curses. When the leaders reached their destination in the West Bank, the demonstrations were larger and more unruly. Carter sympathized with the Palestinians, especially when he saw the high-rise cities on the West Bank erected by Jewish settlers. He publicly criticized Begin for failing to commit to the United Nations Resolution 242, which called for withdrawal of Israelis from territories seized in 1967.

The next stop on their trip was Jordan, where they were welcomed graciously by King Hussein and Queen Nor. Hussein was overwhelmed by Palestinian militants who used Jordanian refugee camps as bases for their frequent attacks on Israel. Carter told Hussein he hoped Jordan would enter into negotiations with Israel. He stated bluntly that the Israeli settlements in the West Bank were "a direct violation of international law and the most serious adverse development [in the region] in the past two years." He also met with King Fahd of Saudi Arabia. At the end of their meetings, Fahd pledged Saudi Arabia's participation in an upcoming discussion at a Middle East consultation led by Carter.

Carter also met with Hafez al-Assad, president of Syria, a known brutal dictator. Washington reacted with intense criticism. How could Jimmy Carter, who professed to be a man of peace, spend time with a dictator like al-Assad? One reporter answered the question: "I've seen Carter sit for an hour with Assad and listen patiently, not saying a word. Then he would finally speak

up, summarizing brilliantly and offering workable solutions to aspects of the inflammatory issue at hand."
By the end of the visit, each man respected the other,
thanks to Carter's patient face-to-face diplomacy.

Carter reported seeing from a plane over Lebanon
the most shattered country in the world. Since 1975,
when civil war erupted in Lebanon, the country had
scarcely known a period without battles, massacres,
raids, and hostage-taking by Israelis, Syrians, Christian
Phalangists, and the PLO. President Amin Gemayel welcomed Jimmy Carter, and together they discussed the
possibility that the United Nations might help create a
lasting peace there.

Carter's trip showed Americans, as well as citizens
and leaders of other countries, he was a man who wanted
to make a difference. In the Middle East, he had been
received with respect, and for the most part, with understanding by leaders of each of the seven countries
he visited. Everywhere he went, he left a message that
he was available as a peacemaker whenever called upon.
He also requested the leaders of these countries contribute funding for the planned Carter Center.

In 1983, architects began building the Carter Center.
By 1984, the Center had hosted a Middle East consultation, a symposium on arms control negotiation, a symposium on world use of natural resources, and a consultation on health policies in the United States. The goals
of the health symposium were to convince Americans to
alter their poor health habits, and to investigate how the
Carter Center could help them to do so. Personally, the

Carters exercised daily and ate low fat, low salt, low cholesterol food. Jimmy stood five foot eight inches tall, and kept his weight at a consistent 165 pounds. The conference also included information on unintended pregnancy, youth homicide, infant mortality, chronic depression, and alcohol abuse. When the center reported that smoking was a contributing factor in half of all deaths in the United States, Carter denounced the tobacco companies as drug pushers.

Concerned that United States-Soviet conflicts might pose a threat to peace, Carter sponsored a forum at the center focusing on Reagan's Strategic Defense Initiative (SDI) that Reagan said would remove the threat of massive nuclear retaliation. SDI, nicknamed "Star Wars" after a Hollywood science-fiction blockbuster, was a massive defense program purported to be capable of stopping missiles aimed at the United States by intercepting them after they had been launched. Speaking

The Carter Center was established to resolve international and national disputes using the conflict resolution method. *(Courtesy of the Carter Center.)*

from his background as a navy officer, Carter gave his opinion of this method of defense. He concluded, "Star Wars is a scam," saying the only benefit from such a scheme would go to the American defense contractors who stood to make millions. Most of the other participants at the conference agreed with Carter's assessment of SDI.

For several years, the Carters had heard about a Georgia-based organization called Habitat for Humanity that built homes for needy people. Neither Jimmy nor Rosalynn paid much attention to the organization until they noted a steady influx of Habitat volunteers in their church in Americus. The leader of the group asked Jimmy and Rosalynn to join their workforce, at least for a day, as an example to potential volunteers. After one day, which began with devotions and proceeded to house-building, the Carters were hooked on the idea. With other couples, they boarded a bus in Americus and traveled a thousand miles to New York City. For over a week, volunteers sawed, hammered, cleaned, and scraped to renovate housing for lower income people. The story of the renovation spread like wildfire, and extensive press coverage brought more volunteers and thousands of dollars to Habitat. The Carters became avid volunteers for the group, and offered to go anywhere and do anything to help the cause. On his sixtieth birthday, Carter asked friends to write a check for Habitat instead of buying him a gift. He chaired a ten million dollar fund-raising campaign for Habitat.

The Carter Center took on a new focus when Carter

Jimmy and Rosalynn Carter became strong advocates for Habitat for Humanity, an organization that builds homes for poor people. *(Courtesy of AP/World Wide Photos.)*

invited Dr. William Foege, a long-time medical missionary and a worker at the Center for Disease Control, to lead an exploration of international health issues. Foege's work at the center was dedicated to children's health problems, especially the 33.5 million children worldwide who died each year from vaccine-preventable diseases like measles, diphtheria, and tuberculosis. Foege nicknamed his inoculation program a "Shot of Love." Within a few weeks of a volcano eruption in Columbia, Carter was on the scene, in jeans and a locally-made shirt, with a vaccine injector in his hand.

He embodied the active participation he demanded of workers at the Carter Center. He warned them they must not simply become paper-pushers. When he gave a deadline, he punctuated it with, "Will we have planted a grain of wheat/corn, delivered a bushel to a hungry family, or initiated an African government change?" To emphasize his attack on bureaucracy and jargon, he said the information that went out from the Center should be in language every peanut farmer could understand.

Carter soon turned his attention to Africa, where more than one hundred million people were malnourished. This might have seemed an impossible situation, especially when reports showed that the population of the continent would triple in fifty years. Carter would not accept as impossible any situation where human lives and minimum standards of living were involved. Under the leadership of agronomist Norman Borlaug, winner of the 1970 Nobel Peace Prize for breeding high-yield dwarf wheat, the Carter Center accepted the challenge to fight famine in African countries.

A visit to Africa convinced the leaders of the Carter Center their focus should be on bringing modern farming techniques to rural districts. Their project would demonstrate new planting and cultivating methods to small farmers. It would center on hand-held tools, contour plowing to reduce erosion, and effective use of fertilizers. Carter hoped to show farmers how to triple their harvest in just one year. Borlaug started the project in Ghana, a west African nation on the Atlantic Ocean. Carter suggested the second target be Sudan, the largest country in Africa, where a civil war raged, three-quarters of the people were illiterate, and an inadequate health care system could not control the spread of yellow fever and cholera.

His plans for Africa were still in the works when Carter felt compelled to enlist the help of the Carter Center in Central America. For decades, United States policy toward Central America had focused on limiting the threat of communism rather than instilling true democracy. Powerful, elite government groups in the area had refused to allow grass-roots participation toward meaningful social and economic reform. Both private investment and government aid from the United States reinforced these governments that suppressed their middle and lower classes. Because of this support for repressive regimes, the hostility of revolutionaries toward the United States grew.

Aware of gross violations of human rights in Central America, the Carters planned to tour the region in February 1986. Reagan administration officials told Carter he must not talk to government leaders without express direction and approval from American diplomats. Carter was determined to follow that warning only as long as it did not interfere with his and the Carter Center's goal of bringing human rights to people everywhere. He would not visit Central America as a rubber stamp for the United States' administration.

The trip proved to be more difficult than Carter had foreseen. In Guatemala, center staff could see no way in which the Carter Center could work with the government to institute reform. In Nicaragua, President Daniel Ortega agreed to release two political prisoners and to consider a full-scale meeting at the Carter Center. In El Salvador, an embattled country on the Pacific coast, Carter needed extra police protection when angry protestors met him at the airport. He saw almost immediately that the state of the civil war in that country would prevent work with the center. In Mexico, the American government posed problems to Carter's visit. The American ambassador insisted on being present when Carter spoke with the Mexican president. Carter refused to visit under this condition.

Back in the United States, Carter summarized his trip as somewhat fruitful. First, it was fruitful because he had reinforced his commitment to peace and justice in the eyes of Central America and the world. Also, he had made personal contacts and given offers of help that he hoped would be accepted at some later time.

The downside of Carter's travels to Central America was the increased hostility directed toward Carter from the Reagan administration. This hostility deepened when the International Court of Justice found the United States in breach of international law because the Reagan administration had been secretly selling arms to Iran and diverting some of the proceeds to the rebels in Nicaragua, known as contras. This situation became known as the Iran-contra affair.

Chapter Eight

New Opportunities

One of Carter's strengths was his ability to move easily from one project to another, from one country to another, from one cause to another. After the Central America trip, he initiated the first annual Jimmy Carter Work Project, a house-building initiative to be held at a different place in the country each summer. In one week, volunteers in the initiative built a complete four-unit townhouse in Chicago. Working side by side with former presidential advisor Charles Colson, a member of the Nixon team who had served time in prison for his part in the Watergate crimes, Carter learned the United States had more prisoners in jail than any other nation. He established an outreach program in which prisoners in Mississippi could be furloughed to join the Habitat group to help build houses. He expanded on the idea of prisoners working for the public by arranging they work part-time for the National Park Service on buildings and grounds projects.

At an international health conference in April 1986, Carter learned about the guinea worm that flourished during droughts in Third World countries. A person could become infected by the worm from drinking stagnant water. The worm could lie in the body for a year or more before bursting thorough the skin, secreting a poison that led to a disease that brought debilitating fever, blisters, and eventually death. Told that only political will was lacking to eradicate the worm, Carter attacked the problem. He engaged the help of the World Health Organization, a specialized agency of the United Nations, to clean up the water supply in afflicted countries. Peace Corps and the United Nations Children's Fund (UNICEF) volunteers taught villagers to build deep wells and to use cloth filters that they distributed. Carter solicited funds for the project from international banks, private philanthropists, and leaders of developing countries that were plagued by the disease.

At a conference at the Carter Center in November 1986, Carter was elected chairman of the Council of Freely Elected Heads of Government. This new organization was composed of elder statesmen, and former and current presidents and prime ministers from Central America, South America, and the Caribbean. They joined together to reinforce democracy, promote conflict resolution, and advance regional economic cooperation.

Around this time, the Carter's eighteen-year-old daughter, Amy, made news when she was arrested for protesting against the apartheid policy of racial segregation in Johannesburg, capital of South Africa. A few months later, she demonstrated against Brown University, where she was a student. The demonstrators demanded Brown divest itself of the $32.5 million invested in companies that dealt with South Africa. In 1986, Amy was in the news thirteen times for protesting against U.S. policy in South Africa and Nicaragua, and against world hunger. Amy described one of the demonstrations, "There were, I would say, sixty or eighty cops in riot gear, billy clubs, Mace, with four or five police dogs." Her parents fully supported her activism.

Requests for help poured into the Carter Center. American missionaries asked for political help to keep churches open in other countries. Organizers requested financial assistance to open an AIDS clinic in San Francisco. Elementary schools asked for money to buy sports equipment. It seemed the requests for help were endless, and some people on the Carter staff complained that Carter took on too many commitments. They said he should prioritize so that, for example, a visit from the head of a county chamber of commerce did not take precedence over a meeting with a national security advisor. Carter refused to prioritize in this way. In his mind, an hour was an hour, and in the eyes of God, all people were equal.

The Carter Center's project to fight hunger in Africa moved a large step ahead in 1986 when the center opened an agricultural project office in Accra, the capital of Ghana. For the foundation of his project there, Carter used the report on the future of the world environment called Global 2000, a report he had commissioned while president. Two one-acre demonstration plots were given to respected local farmers. On one of these plots, the farmers were to use traditional techniques, and on the other, to use improved seed and some nitrogen fertilizer. The results of the demonstration dramatically proved the advantages of modern farming methods, and a "Green Revolution" was launched in Ghana.

Carter hoped to extend this Green Revolution to Zimbabwe, a country in southeastern Africa. But at a reception congratulating the United States on its 210th birthday, the foreign minister of Zimbabwe denounced Reagan. In reaction to this insult, the Carters walked out of the reception, along with diplomats from other nations. Zimbabwe President Robert Mugabe apologized to Carter and Reagan for the remarks made by his foreign minister. Carter wrote to Mugabe expressing his hopes that the Carter Center agricultural initiative would be supported there. Reagan announced that no new United States economic aid would be sent to Zimbabwe because of the insolence of the foreign minister. Carter remarked he might have stayed around after the insult to see if there was a way to ease the situation if he had known Reagan would react this severely.

Carter once again turned his attention to the Soviets. After talking with many diplomats, Carter came to believe the Russians wanted to reduce their nuclear weapons and would if they could do so without appearing to back down to the United States. He initiated another consultation at the Carter Center and met with Soviet Ambassador to the United States Anatoly Dobrynin before the meetings began. By the opening of the conference, Carter knew both Dobrynin and the new Soviet premier Mikhail Gorbachev would go along with the proposal.

The meeting proceeded smoothly with Carter and Gerald Ford co-chairing the event. The two former presidents steered the meetings to productive talk despite the open conflict and hostility between the Americans and the Soviets. Before the meeting ended, the Soviets had agreed to stop nuclear testing and to allow on-site inspection of some of their radar and missile facilities if Reagan would scrap the SDI initiative. Both sides agreed to continue meeting about reduction of armaments. Told about the meeting, Reagan said he would not agree based on the terms of SALT II nor would he negotiate on any aspect of SDI.

The release of prisoners of conscience, also called political prisoners, was an ongoing concern of the Carter Center. The center's approach to this problem was to have Carter speak directly to the leaders suspected of violating human rights by imprisoning these political dissidents. It is estimated Carter was responsible for freeing over fifty thousand such prisoners between 1981 and 1997, accomplishing most of the releases through his personal communications with political leaders. Among the countries whose record on human rights Carter questioned were Haiti, Tunisia, Thailand, the Soviet Union, and Israel.

In 1987, the Jimmy Carter Presidential Library opened. Visitors were astounded at the number of Carter documents housed there—about 27.5 million. Carter had been one of the most prolific memo writers in the history of the presidency. Visitors were also surprised at the extent of Carter's involvement in policy matters.

In 1987, Carter wrote in *Time* magazine that he saw new opportunities for peace in the Middle East and urged greater American involvement in the process. He announced he was going to visit the area again and would report back to the United States on what he found there. The United States administration warned him not to speak to the heads of government of Syria or the PLO. Carter traveled with two itineraries. One was for the State Department and discussed his travels as Professor Carter of Emory University. The other itinerary was for Carter's staff and included visits to Yasir Arafat's emissaries in Jordan and to Assad's cabinet in Syria. He was warmly welcomed in Egypt, Jordan, and Syria, countries at odds with the Reagan administration.

Jimmy and Rosalynn Carter took a Global 2000 initiative to Thailand, where they laid a cornerstone for a shelter for abused women, and to China, where they signed agreements to develop programs for the training of handicapped people. They promised support for new technologies for the manufacture of artificial limbs.

Next Carter turned his attention to river blindness, a debilitating condition caused by a parasitic worm found primarily in Africa. The parasite breeds in swiftly moving streams, and people who use the contaminated water for drinking, bathing, and fishing come into contact with the worm. Several years after being infected, the victim may lose his sight due to eye infections. Estimates in parts of central and east Africa were that sixty-two percent of people over fifty-five were blind. Research scientists in New Jersey discovered that a single pill of the type used to combat heartworm could prevent or arrest river blindness. The Merck pharmaceutical company, manufacturers of this pill, called Mectizan, agreed to donate the pill for as long as it was needed to fight the disease. Carter made plans to oversee the delivery and distribution of Mectizan through the Carter Center.

The Middle East again demanded his attention when a wave of riots broke out. Palestinians engaged in general strikes, boycotts, tire burning, and stone throwing against Israelis. Israeli Defense Minister Yitzhak Rabin answered with military troops. Photos of young Pales-

Jimmy and Rosalynn touring the Carter Presidential Center in Atlanta. *(Courtesy of UPI/ Bettman News Photos.)*

tinians standing against thousands of well-armed Israeli soldiers drew massive international condemnation of Rabin. The Camp David Accords lost their impact.

On the domestic scene, Ronald Reagan could not run for re-election in the 1988 campaign since he had already served two terms. Vice President George Herbert Walker Bush ran against Democratic candidate Governor Michael Dukakis of Massachusetts. Part of Bush's campaign warned against a Democratic presidency, citing Carter's record of twenty–one percent interest rates, double-digit inflation, high unemployment, and block-long lines for gasoline. Bush won the election.

The new Bush administration asked Carter to head a delegation to Panama to monitor the upcoming election there. At stake was the election of Carlos Duque, a candidate chosen by General Manual Noriega, who was the real power in the country. Reports from Panama indicated Noriega was engaging in widespread threats, coercion, and fraud to ensure the election of government officials who would continue to support him.

Carter wrote to Noriega warning, "As I have been critical of the U.S. government for some of its policies toward Panama, I too will feel compelled to protest an unfair election in Panama." After some blustering about not needing monitors, Noriega agreed to let Carter and twenty monitors oversee the election. He complained about Carter's request for a visa. "How can a great statesman like Jimmy Carter speak of visas? But if he wants a visa, we will give him one eternally."

During the campaign, monitors presented Noriega with evidence of press censorship, intimidation and fraud. Noriega answered that the Reagan-Bush administrations had funded opposition candidates and he was only fighting back.

When Carter arrived at the airport in Panama, he made a speech declaring that he hoped to see Panama work towards becoming a democracy. He spoke in Spanish on radio and television shows, begging voters to cast ballots. "Come out and vote. I want to see you." Fifty thousand volunteers spread out over the polling stations to make sure the votes were accurately tabulated. Three-quarters of the eligible voters went to the polls. By early morning, a representative sampling of polling places reported that Noriega's opponent had won, perhaps by a margin of three to one. Before the voting was finished, Noriega shut down the polls and ordered his staff to seize votes, at gun point if necessary.

The new Panamanian administration asked Carter to help them face Noriega. Carter's reputation for honesty and fairness was well known in Panama, and so was his unique ability to find a common ground through face-to-face meetings with a person who had been reluctant to yield to other pressures. Carter agreed, but Noriega refused. Washington asked Carter to present to Noriega a plan under which Noriega would be helped to exile in Spain if he accepted the results of the election. Carter wanted to do this, but Noriega would not talk with him. Carter wondered if he could have helped Noriega to accept the results of the election better if he had spent more time establishing mutual trust before the election.

When Carter saw that Panamanian government bureaucrats were falsifying voting tabulation records, he scheduled a press conference to report what he had seen. Armed with bayonets, Noriega's soldiers locked the conference hall where the international press assembled. Carter held the conference in the lobby of a hotel and proclaimed, "The government is taking the election by fraud . . . I hope there will be a worldwide outcry against the dictator who stole this election from his own people." Carter was seen around the world as a positive force for peace and justice.

That night, Noriega sent tanks into the streets and nullified the election. Carter flew to Washington to urge President Bush to use international pressure, not military intervention, to remove Noriega from the country. Bush rejected Carter's suggestion. He deployed troops to regions outside the Panama Canal area and added twelve thousand troops to those permanently stationed in Panama.

Chapter Nine

Promoting Democracy

When Carter felt he could do no more in Panama, he turned his attention to the thirty-year-long civil war in Ethiopia in northeastern Africa. Since 1974, more than half a million people had died there due to widespread famine and civil war. Ethiopia was the world's poorest country at the time, with a per capita income of $120 a year, only one-fifth of the children in school, and a lack of clean drinking water for ninety-four percent of the population. In September 1989, the Carter Center announced a peace summit in Atlanta to attempt to end the country's civil war.

Carter was not the first to try to stop the bloodshed in Ethiopia. He was, however, the first to approach the talks determined that the countries would succeed in fashioning a solution to their problems. With his typical attention to research and study, Carter made three trips to Ethiopia before he opened the talks. He became knowledgeable about the problems of food distribution, and he convinced Ethiopia's President Mengistu Haile Mariam it would it be in his best interest to talk with Isaias Afwerki, the leader of his opponents.

The meetings started with no preconditions. Rather they opened with the parties themselves deciding issues of procedural rules and agendas. Carter made it clear to the participants that these decisions were in their hands. Nothing would be imposed on them. Working with a laptop, Carter kept a record of issues discussed and language used throughout the meetings.

When American staff took time off for Thanksgiving, the Carters moved the talks to Nairobi, Kenya. To share an American Thanksgiving, he and Rosalynn served turkey and gourd pie for guests. They joined hands for Christian prayers, and they taught some country gospel songs. This made news throughout Africa, and Africans were impressed with the commitment of the ex-president and with his stamina. His Secret Service agents, too, were impressed, especially those who dropped from exhaustion while trying to keep up with Carter's daily five-mile runs.

The talks continued in Africa, and were sometimes so tense Carter had to meet with each side separately. Ultimately, he achieved cease-fires in Ethiopia but did not secure a lasting peace. Carter summed up the results of the talks: "We still helped to achieve a cease-fire in the country for over a year—and let the different groups begin to understand and acknowledge one another, a crucial step for the eventual democratization of the country." With these words, Carter summarized his philosophy that acceptance of and respect for one another is the key to peace and justice.

Meanwhile, in Panama, Noriega had returned to his strong-arm methods of controlling the nation. American soldiers in Panama were routinely harassed. A United States marine lieutenant was killed, a second soldier wounded, and another detained and beaten after his car failed to stop at a roadblock. In retaliation, Bush and his advisors decided to invade Panama. Forty-eight hours after this decision was made, ten thousand United States troops backed by gunships and fighter bombers advanced into Panama. The air force dropped over four hundred bombs in thirteen hours. Less than two weeks after the soldiers invaded, Noriega surrendered. He was helicoptered to an air force base in America and delivered into the custody of the United States. Carter criticized the United States' invasion as a violation of international law and Panamanian sovereignty. The United Nations General Assembly agreed the invasion was a violation of international law. In the United States, however, over three-quarters of the people called the American attack justified, and this gave Bush's foreign policy an assuredness that would surface a year later in the Persian Gulf War.

An ex-president does not have to be concerned with party loyalties, and Carter made the most of this freedom. Just as he had collaborated with Republican Gerald Ford in election monitoring, now he worked with James Baker, Bush's secretary of state. With the goal of promoting democracy abroad, the two men made significant contributions in Panama, Haiti, the Dominican Republic, Guyana, Suriname, Zambia, and Nicaragua. Baker noted their collaboration was a fine piece of bipartisan cooperation. He also applauded the fact that their work took the foreign policy of Central America out of the domestic debate in America.

Carter continued his work in Central America, where he was asked to monitor the upcoming presidential elections in Nicaragua. Carter asked the Council of Freely Elected Heads of Government to station three full-time staffers in Nicaragua to monitor the six-month campaign that would precede the election. A team of fifty observers went there with Carter before the election to meet officials and learn about the ballots and voting methods. They sponsored a mass voter registration drive, but this campaign was marred by intimidation and violence. Carter tried to calm both sides by sending election inspectors to rallies and by stressing the importance of a free and fair election.

On election day, Nicaragua, with a population of only about five million, teemed with around five thousand observers. When he learned Ortega had been defeated, Carter told him, "Your greatest accomplishment as president will be if you lead a peaceful transition of power."

After monitoring an election in the Dominican Republic, a country in the Caribbean, Carter returned to the United States and quickly became involved in another African project. The Carter Center International Task Force for Disease Eradication announced that an

American company had donated over two and a half million dollars to make guinea worm eradication possible within five years. Throughout the United States, some people wondered publicly why the Carter Center would be involved in such a massive project in a foreign country. Carter explained that time and money spent on the guinea worm problem now would reduce the need for humanitarian aid in the long run.

In July 1990, Carter was asked to monitor campaigns in Haiti for the December election. In the months before the election, dissidents used inflammatory speeches and death threats against candidates. They killed seven people and injured fifty others. Carter called in observers from the United Nations, the Organization of American States (OAS), the United States, and other countries. The result was a smooth election day. The victor, Father Aristide, a thirty-seven-year-old Catholic priest, won with two-thirds of the vote. Carter announced the election in Haiti would give hope to all countries in the hemisphere. His hopes were short-lived. After only seven months in office, the military toppled the government and Aristide fled, first to Venezuela and then to America.

Regarding the Middle East, Carter had made it clear he thought face-to-face contact with Arafat was the next logical step toward resolution of the ongoing Israeli-Palestinian conflict. When Bush gave Carter permission to talk with Arafat, he required Carter to report to American officials after each meeting. When reporters asked why he would talk to a known terrorist, Carter reminded questioners that both Yitzak Shamir and Menachem Begin, former prime ministers of Israel, had once been members of underground Jewish terrorist organizations and were now considered peacemakers. He said he assumed it would be possible for Arafat also to change his attitudes.

After a thorough review of the situation, Carter showed documentation proving Israelis had jailed nine thousand Palestinians without trials and killed six hundred fifty Palestinians with unjustified use of firearms by the military. Although many criticized Carter for a pro-Palestinian bias for these comments, he refused to back down.

He met with Arafat in Paris with no reporters present. Arafat brought eight of his supporters. Carter brought Rosalynn and one aide. When Carter opened the session saying he came as a private citizen, not as a spokesman for the United States government, Arafat responded, "Yes, but you bring strong moral power."

Parts of the charter that established the PLO referred to the necessity of an armed struggle and for the elimination of the State of Israel. Carter asked Arafat to remove these provisions from the charter. In return, he promised the PLO would be given membership in the World Health Organization as well as provided access to high-ranking U.S. officials. When Arafat agreed to meet these conditions, Carter then asked him to publicly endorse the agreements made at Camp David between Sadat and Begin. Arafat agreed. Jimmy, Rosalynn, and Arafat wept, embraced, and prayed together. Soon after that meeting, Arafat wrote to Carter asking if he would convene an international peace conference and stated his willingness to participate. Carter eagerly agreed.

Hopes for a Middle East settlement plummeted on August 1, 1990, when ten thousand Iraqi troops invaded Kuwait, a country the size of New Jersey bordered on the north and west by Iraq. Within hours, Iraqi dictator Saddam Hussein announced the annexation of Kuwait, citing historical rights to the territory. In response, the United Nations Security Council adopted a comprehensive embargo against Iraq. President Bush announced the United States would declare war on Iraq if it did not leave Kuwait by January 15. He cited Iraq's invasion of Kuwait and its possession of conventional, chemical, biological, and nuclear weapons, which were a serious threat to world peace. Bush justified his actions with the Carter Doctrine that stated any attempt by an outside force to gain control of the Persian Gulf Region would be considered an assault on the vital interests of America.

Carter said he would prefer to work toward peace without setting a deadline. That fall, he pursued negotiations in face-to-face meetings with officials. He wrote many persuasive articles in magazines and newspapers as well. Everywhere he criticized the Bush plans and recited the history of recent military involvement of the United States, emphasizing, "In none of these cases, did we first exhaust the opportunities for peaceful resolution of the dispute." He wrote to heads of state of UN

Security Council members and asked them to hold good faith negotiations with Hussein before entering into a war against him. He sent the same letter to other heads of state whom he believed could exert influence in the UN General Assembly. He asked them to abandon support for the United States and give support instead to the Arab League, a voluntary association of twenty-one nations. The Bush administration was outraged by his suggestions, and called him a "peace outlaw."

On January 12, 1991, Congress approved Bush's request for a resolution supporting the use of force in Iraq. On January 17, United States troops invaded Iraq with a full-scale attack known as Operation Desert Storm. Less than two months later, Kuwait was liberated, and Bush announced a cease-fire.

Carter and Bush were on opposite sides in another international situation. From his base at the Carter Center, Aristide pushed for his return to Haiti as the first freely elected president in the history of his country. Both he and Carter were concerned about the thousands of Haitians who had fled Haiti, many in unseaworthy boats headed for the Florida Keys. The United States had ordered the refugees to return, saying they were not fleeing legally for political asylum but because they wanted to better themselves economically. Carter declared this condemnation was an affront to United States law and to the New Testament. He said the United States had a moral duty to help the refugees since Haiti suffered with a sixty percent unemployment rate, an AIDS epidemic, and a growing number of poor and homeless.

"Bush acted as if the Haitians weren't people," Carter said. He declared Bush would not have had the same answer if the refugees had been white.

In October 1991, Jimmy Carter initiated the Atlanta Project "to prove that in at least one troubled city something can be done about the problem of teenage pregnancy, drug addiction, and crack babies, juvenile delinquents, homelessness, and unemployment." The funding would come from private foundations and the business community, not from taxes. He was determined this program would do more than simply provide benefits to the needy; it would create permanent changes in living conditions. Large companies like Coca-Cola, Delta Airlines, Turner Broadcasting Systems, and United Parcel Service gave both money and moral support. One of Carter's first initiatives was to simplify the red tape necessary to obtain assistance. He asked for the creation of an easy-to-complete form, preferably one-page, for an application for food stamps, Medicare, and housing assistance.

Chapter Ten

Committed and Tireless

In the 1992 Presidential election, the winning candidate was Arkansas's Democratic Governor Bill Clinton, who had chosen as his running mate Tennessee Senator Al Gore. Six weeks after Clinton's inauguration, Carter and his aides met with Clinton's new secretary of state, Warren Christopher. Carter said he wanted to be involved in attempts to further peace and democracy in Liberia, Haiti, Ethiopia, Somalia, Cuba, and the Middle East. He told Christopher he could talk easily and effectively to the heads of governments in those places because he already had a track record there. Christopher said, "I appreciate your offer, Mr. President, but as you know in most cases we're going to have to take the lead."

Carter was not discouraged from the goals he had set for himself at the opening of the Carter Center. He was encouraged by results such as those in Ghana where, six years after the first Carter Center projects were initiated, that country held its first democratic election for president in thirty years. For Carter, this was the fulfillment of his two-part plan. First, he had won entry into the country with agricultural assistance, and then he had pushed for democratic elections. In the Sudan, his goals met with less success. The center made significant inroads at first, but civil conflicts between Moslems and Christians kept the country in chaos. Carter worked tirelessly to achieve a cease-fire. Although he was unable to achieve this, it was through his efforts that wheat production rose from about 150,000 tons in 1987 to 830,000 tons in 1992, relieving some of Sudan's food shortage problems.

Despite the comments of Secretary of State Christopher, President Clinton asked Carter for suggestions about the Haitian refugees. Carter did not trust Aristide

President Bill Clinton, pictured with his wife Hillary, asked for Carter's assistance dealing with the conflict in Haiti. *(Courtesy of AP Photo.)*

as a proponent of democracy. He had heard reports from Amnesty International that Aristide had condoned "necklacing"—putting a tire around a victim's neck and setting it on fire. Still, true to his commitment to the outcome of free and fair elections, Carter advocated Aristide be installed as the duly elected president of Haiti. He recommended Aristide first promise to guarantee human rights to all citizens. Clinton preferred to use a United Nations option which allowed individual member states to use force to restore a constitutional government. He deployed a U.S. aircraft carrier off the shores of Florida.

The leader of the coup that toppled Aristide, General Raoul Cédras, signaled to Carter that he wanted to talk peace with him. When told about the offer, the Clinton administration told Carter not to go. The United States government set a deadline. If Cédras were still in office in three weeks on September 19, the United States would invade Haiti. Carter convinced United States officials that Cédras was so desperate at this time, and so unpopular with Haitians, the State Department could offer him a face-saving departure without resorting to armed conflict. He asked to be the messenger, and with reluctant administration approval, he traveled to Haiti on September 17.

In the early afternoon of September 18, Carter faxed the White House an agreement in which Cédras would step down from office but would not leave the country. Aristide insisted he would not return to office if Cédras were free in Haiti.

Just before 4:00 P.M. that same day, the number-two man in Cédras's administration burst into the negotiating room. He told Carter to leave immediately because an American military force was heading for Haiti. Carter refused to yield to the threat. He had Cédras's signature on an agreement that would allow 250,000 U.S. troops to work with the Haitian military and to elect a new parliament in a democratic election. In return for this, the United States would lift economic sanctions. Carter was sure this contract would halt the planned U.S. invasion once it was signed by Haiti's provisional president, Emile Jonaissant, and received the approval of President Clinton.

As the mediators rushed to the Presidential Palace and got Jonaissant's signature, planes were loading troops from American bases. Carter called Clinton and received the go-ahead to sign the agreement for him. At 6:00 P.M., Carter called Clinton to tell him the agreement was properly signed.

Carter was asleep on the plane back to Washington when he learned the invasion had been merely postponed, not canceled. One hundred forty helicopters would land in Haiti the next day at 10:00 A.M. to take Cédras into exile. Carter intervened, saying such a move would be a violation of Cédras's human rights. He hurriedly made contacts with a friend in Panama City who agreed to take Cédras to Panama. On October 15, Cédras was in Panama when Aristide returned to office.

On his seventieth birthday, Carter was awarded the J. William Fulbright Prize for International Understanding. Many people rushed to congratulate him. Others wondered why he had failed to win the more prestigious Nobel Peace Prize.

He was seventy years old and had won a highly respected award, but Carter was not finished with his mission for peace. He turned his attention to Bosnia, in the former country of Yugoslavia, where multi-ethnic diversity became ethnic hostility in 1992 when Eastern Orthodox Serbians, Catholic Croatians, and Bosnian Muslims all laid claim to the government. Reports from the area were full of ghastly reports of "ethnic cleansing," mass rapes, and genocide. In February 1994, Clinton called on NATO to protect Bosnian Muslims, and two months later, NATO jets were bombing Bosnia. In capitulation, Radovan Karadzic, a Bosnian Serb warlord, agreed to open the closed airport at the capital city of Sarajevo, allow humanitarian flights, allow freedom of movement to United Nations peacekeepers, release all Muslim prisoners under nineteen years old, and impose a four-month cease-fire on the condition that Carter visit him.

Carter agreed with no hesitation, rejecting warnings from Clinton's administration that Karadzic only wanted to use the former president to protect himself. "My view was that there wasn't much of a peace process anyway," Carter said. He did not excuse the crimes committed by Bosnian leaders, but he believed any settlement of the conflict was contingent on talking with the people involved.

In Bosnia, the Carters were appalled by the destruction caused by the conflict. Bridges and buildings were razed, and rubble was everywhere. Rosalynn described the scene: "Graves, graves, graves . . . thousands and thousands of them, all over the city . . . the Olympic Stadium is totally demolished, the Town Hall is destroyed. Remains of summer vegetable plots along the streets: garbage everywhere."

The Carters met first with President Alija Izetbegovic, head of the Muslim-dominated government, who seemed agreeable to Carter's ideas. Then they met with Karadzic, who accepted the Carter draft for a cease-fire. Carter returned to Izetbegovic for his signature. Izetbegovic refused to sign a cease-fire unless Karadzic agreed to accept a plan giving forty-nine percent of Bosnia to Serbs and fifty-one percent to the Muslim-Croat Federation. Karadzic refused. Carter persuaded Izetbegovic to accept the document with no mention of the division of land.

Carter called the White House and told officials Karadzic had agreed to a four-month cease-fire. He was told the U.S. State Department condemned the Carter Center mission since the Bosnian Serbs were at that moment shelling a United Nations-designated safe zone. Surprised, Carter asked Karadzic to have the shelling stopped, and Karadzic said he would. The next morning, Karadzic said he would not stop the shelling. Carter spoke with Karadzic again, and again Karadzic agreed to accept the nationwide cease-fire and pledged to resume peace talks just as Izetbegovic had done.

As news of the cease-fire spread, Carter critics said

it was a white flag of surrender. They accused the former president of making deals with a war criminal. Many said the cease-fire would not last. They were right. From the moment the document was signed, sporadic fighting took place.

In April, Serb forces took several hundred UN peace-keepers hostage and shot down American pilots. In July, thousands of Muslims were killed in Bosnia. NATO staged air strikes against Bosnian Serb military targets. At one point, Karadzic assured Carter he would withdraw his heavy artillery from Sarajevo. He failed to keep that promise. NATO military forces brought the enemies to the negotiating table. On October 5, another Bosnian cease-fire was announced. Clinton called for a summit in Dayton, Ohio. In December, the meeting in Dayton resulted in a peace accord. Although he was not a part of the negotiations, Carter expressed satisfaction that the Clinton officials conducted the talks using a conflict resolution model.

Carter continued to amaze those who watched him closely. He appeared resolute and seemingly tireless. He was unremitting in his determination to make peace at any price, even if meant forgoing judging those who caused the suffering. He saw confirmation of this philosophy when he received a handwritten message from Arafat asking for a meeting at once. Arafat told Carter that he and Rabin had come to an agreement in Oslo at a secret meeting spearheaded by Norway's Institute of Applied Sciences. He said they would sign letters of mutual agreement on September 9 in Paris and asked

Carter to help win Clinton's approval of the deal. Carter promised to do so.

A White House ceremony celebrating the Oslo agreement signing was scheduled for September 13. Carter met with Arafat the night before the ceremony. When Arafat told him he planned to move to Jericho or Gaza within two months, Carter said, "We all owe you a debt of gratitude, you have been so patient and so wise."

The next morning, Foreign Minister Shimon Perez of Israel and Mahmoud Abbas of the PLO signed the agreement called the Declaration of Principles. Both Israel and the PLO acknowledged the right of the other to exist as sovereign nations. The Israelis agreed to accept the results of elections in Gaza, and the PLO agreed to concede Jerusalem to Israel. The PLO was recognized as the representative of the Palestinian people. The foreign minister from Yemen noted later he had seen a tear roll down Carter's cheek when the signing was completed.

Carter met with Arafat, who told him the World Bank had refused to send him the funds he had been led to expect. Arafat contended that for signing the agreement Israel had been richly rewarded with computer systems, F-15s, sixty-five million dollars for deployment from Gaza, and other massive grants. Arafat said he received nothing and was treated as a pariah, not a peacemaker. Carter promised to call the World Bank and write a public opinion piece to put pressure on all the funding groups involved. Carter suggested part of the problem occurred because a Palestinian radical

Carter met with the president of North Korea, Kim Il Sung. *(Courtesy of the Carter Center.)*

leader refused to promise he would not commit violence against members of the Rabin government. Arafat agreed to get that leader to back down. Both men decided the Carter Center would help with the Palestinian election slated for January 1996.

The next potential emergency on Carter's list arose when the CIA discovered North Korea could produce plutonium, an important component of atomic weapons. The Department of Defense sent fifty thousand troops and anti-missile weapons to South Korea to prepare for a possible attack on North Korea, and it outlined possible sanctions on the country that included cutting United Nations aid. Carter asked the Clinton administration for permission to go to North Korea to defuse the situation. Permission was granted as long as Carter made it clear he was going as a private citizen, not as an emissary of the United States government.

Carter recognized the immediate needs of each side. The United States and the international community wanted North Korea to accept full and regular inspection of their nuclear facilities. North Korea wanted to establish full diplomatic relations with the United States and to receive help modernizing its nuclear program.

After several weeks, Carter called the White House to report there had been a diplomatic breakthrough. He said Kim Il Sung, the president of North Korea, had agreed to allow international inspectors to remain in the country, to dismantle his existing nuclear reactors, and to halt construction of new ones. A condition was that the United States would supply the light-water reactors the North Korean president needed to generate electricity and would drop the idea of imposing sanctions. Washington officials responded that Carter had been gullible to believe Kim Il Sung. They said Kim had tricked him into forestalling sanctions so North Korea would have more time to build up a defense. Carter criticized Clinton's talk of sanctions, saying they would doom all chances of positive relations.

In the first Sunday school class Carter taught after his return, he stated that Christ, like Carter, had been mocked for preaching peace. He spoke highly of the character of Kim Il Sung. Despite its harsh criticisms of the Carter initiative, the United States dropped the push for sanctions and accepted the written confirmation of North Korea's agreement to freeze its nuclear program in return for the delivery of light-water reactors and a gradual return to diplomatic relations.

A few weeks later, Kim Il Sung died of a massive heart attack. A three-year-long official mourning period would take place before his son Kim Jong Il would assume leadership. Carter continued his relationship with North Korea by helping its leaders to successfully negotiate their country's participation in the 1996 Summer Olympics in Atlanta.

Chapter Eleven

We Can Choose

In the first three months of 1995, Carter traveled to six countries and a dozen American cities. He negotiated a cease-fire in Sudan, oversaw the final eradication of the guinea worm in Pakistan, promoted Habitat for Humanity in the underdeveloped world, and agreed to write a monthly column for the *New York Times*. He held conflict resolution meetings, taught Sunday school classes, and worked on his eleventh book—a children's story he wrote with Amy. Ted Turner, an influential television executive, said, "[Carter] does more hard work in a single day than most humans do in a lifetime." Carter commented, "Sometimes, I even have fun doing my duty."

For his next mission, Carter chose Cuba, an island nation just off the southern coast of Florida. In 1960, Cuba expropriated about one billion dollars of United States-owned property. The next year, Cuban rebel troops supported by the United States landed an invasion force in southern Cuba, an act that worsened relations between the countries without adding advantage to either side. In 1962, President Kennedy narrowly avoided an open war when he forced Premier Castro to dismantle Cuban missiles aimed at Florida. The Clinton administration planned to tighten the United States' thirty-three-year old economic embargo against that island nation. Carter predicted the extension of the embargo would limit the possibility of working with Cubans. Clinton sent a message to Carter: Do not meddle in Cuban affairs. Carter backed off publicly, but he told his students at Emory, "We hope you will do something about that [the Cuban situation], but don't tell anybody I told you that."

He kept traveling. In Nigeria, a republic in western Africa, he spoke to head of state General Sani Abacha about the imprisonment of the former president Obasanjo. Abacha had seized power in a military coup in 1993 and had systematically imprisoned, intimidated, and murdered political dissidents. Carter asked him to free political prisoners and to allow unrestricted delivery of the cloth filters needed to eradicate the guinea worm. The Carter Center secured a pledge from Abacha to install a water tank within a month. Abacha permitted Obasanjo to remain at his home under house arrest until charges against him were investigated.

In the Nigerian countryside, the Carters were enthusiastically welcomed. Rosalynn noted that one child held a sign that said: "Guinea worm, you better go away. President Carter is coming." The couple were crowned as honorary chiefs of a village.

Children in Ghana hold up signs welcoming Jimmy and Rosalynn Carter. *(Courtesy of the Carter Center.)*

Back in Washington, Carter's actions generated public opposition. Pro-African democracy groups and a number of prominent African Americans asked how Carter could brag he had freed just one person and obtained a promise for one water tank in Nigeria. They derided him for believing Abacha could be trusted. In the next months, as Abacha's government became even more despotic, Carter admitted he had made a mistake.

Carter kept his promise to Arafat to monitor the first democratic elections ever held for Palestinians. In January 1996, he went to Jerusalem where Arafat and one other candidate were running for the presidency. It looked as though Arafat would easily win a majority of the one million votes since he had handpicked his only opponent, an obscure seventy-two-year-old woman. Although some boycotted the election, turnout was about eighty percent in most places. However, in East Jerusalem, where Israeli police surrounded the polling places, turnout was only about twenty-five percent. Carter complained policemen in riot gear were intimidating voters there. He threatened to call off the elections if the police were not pulled back immediately. They were dispersed, and Arafat won by over eighty percent of the vote.

That election did not end the area's conflict. By March, Palestinian Hamas terrorists had killed fifty-seven Israelis in suicide bombings. Although Arafat denounced the terrorism, world opinion was he could have prevented it. In May, Binyamin Netanyahu was elected Israel's prime minister, and he brought with him a complete rejection of the land-for-peace deal worked out in the Oslo accord.

Carter's record in Africa was much more optimistic. By 1997, the Carter Center had initiated humanitarian programs in twelve African countries. In Sub-Saharan Africa, the Global 2000 program brought new planting techniques and hardier seeds to Ghana, Tanzania, Zambia, Sudan, and Ethiopia. Some Ethiopian farmers reported seeing three and four hundred percent increases in their grain yield. Although many people around the world had given up on Africa, Carter's missionary zeal kept him working steadily to save lives and encourage human rights. He used his African experiences as a lesson to his Sunday school class: "Each of us can honor God through our life's commitment, in our activities, and through giving and sharing our time and talents with others."

Jimmy and Rosalynn Carter monitored elections in Mozambique in December 1999.
(Courtesy of the Carter Center.)

In the next four years, the Carters and the Carter Center monitored elections in China, Venezuela, Nigeria, Oklahoma (the Cherokee Nation elections), Indonesia, Mozambique, Peru, the Dominican Republic, and Mexico.

In 2002, Carter became the first American president to visit Cuba in forty years. From Cuba, Carter sent back word to Washington that Castro had introduced some essential reforms in his government that had led to a more open press, free elections, and greater economic freedom. He said further reform was thwarted by harsh demands from Washington, and he called for the end of the United States trade embargo on Cuba.

That same year, the Carter Center celebrated the

twentieth anniversary of its founding with reports of success in aiding areas of conflict and suffering not addressed by governments or the media. Several center programs were singled out for particular praise, including the International Negotiation Network and the Global Development Initiative. The International Negotiation Network (INN) monitors global conflicts on a weekly basis. The INN also offers assistance to new and struggling democracies. It focuses on the many civil conflicts throughout the world and on solutions for these conflicts.

The Global Development Initiative (GDI) is devoted to economic development that is fiscally, socially, and environmentally sustainable. The Human Rights Program draws attention to victims of human rights abuses and to both governmental and non-governmental organizations that are struggling to protect human rights.

Never in the history of America has there been an ex-president who captured so many headlines and made a difference in so many parts of the world. He redefined the role of ex-president, and proved a former president can contribute significantly to the advancement of humanitarian efforts at home and abroad and to the development of peaceful relations in and among nations.

In October 2002, Jimmy Carter was awarded the Nobel Peace Prize "for his decades of untiring effort to find peaceful solutions to international conflicts, to advance democracy and human rights, and to promote economic and social development . . . Carter has stood by the principles that conflicts must as far as possible

In October 2002, Jimmy Carter received the Nobel Peace Prize.
(Courtesy of AP Photo.)

be resolved through mediation and international cooperation."

When asked by a reporter, "What drives you?" Jimmy Carter answered:

"I don't know . . . exactly how to express it. As I said, it's not an unpleasant sense of being driven. I feel like I have one life to live. I feel like that God wants me to do the best I can with it. And that's quite often my major prayer. Let me live my life so that it will be meaningful. And I enjoy attacking difficult problems and solving of solutions and answering the difficult questions and the meticulous organization of a complicated effort. It's a challenge—possibly it's like a game. I don't know. I don't want to lower it by saying it's just a game but it's an enjoyable thing for me."

In his Nobel Prize acceptance speech, Carter challenged: "God gives us the capacity for choice. We can choose to alleviate suffering. We can choose to work together for peace. We can make those changes—and we must."

Timeline

1924   Born in Plains, Georgia, October 1.

1946   Graduates from U.S. Naval Academy at Annapolis, Maryland; marries Rosalynn.

1953   Returns to Plains, Georgia, to run family business.

1962   Serves in Georgia state senate until 1966.

1970   Elected governor of Georgia.

1976   Elected president of the United States.

1977   Signs Panama Canal treaty.

1979   Signs Camp David Accords.

1980   Presents the "Carter Doctrine;" loses bid for re-election as president.

1982   Founds the Carter Center.

1984   Becomes a member of the board of directors of Habitat for Humanity.

1994   Meets with North and South Korean leaders; facilitates talks between Bosnian Muslims and Serbs.

1996   Monitors Palestinian elections.

1998   Receives first United Nations Human Rights Prize.

1999   With his wife, Rosalynn, wins Presidential Medal of Freedom.

2002   Wins Nobel Peace Prize.

Sources

CHAPTER ONE: Back to Plains

p. 15, "Carter was very well liked . . ." Bruce and Edwin Diamond Mazlish, *Jimmy Carter: A Character Portrait* (New York: Simon & Schuster, 1979), 100.

p. 15, "The only times . . ." Ibid., 99.

p. 18, "Why not?" Peter Bourne, *Jimmy Carter* (New York: A Lisa Drew Book, 1997), 73.

p. 18, "I want to be a man . . ." Mazlish, *Jimmy Carter*, 39.

p. 18, "I argued. I cried . . ." Rosalynn Carter, *First Lady from Plains* (Boston: Houghton Mifflin Company, 1984), 36.

CHAPTER TWO: Learning the Ropes

p. 23, "The law requires . . ." Bourne, *Jimmy Carter*, 119.

p. 23, "Doc [his friend] here is the . . ." Ibid., 119.

p. 23, "Everybody knows . . ." Ibid., 120.

p. 25, "always a reckoning" Bourne, *Character Portrait* (New York: A Lisa Drew Book, 1997), 25.

p. 25, "There will be no integration . . ." PBS American Experience, *Jimmy Carter*.

p. 27, "asked me if I would . . ." Betty Glad, *Jimmy Carter: In Search of the Great White House* (New York: W.W. Norton & Co., 1980), 108.

p. 28, "The sad duty of politics . . ." Burton Kaufman, *The Presidency of James Earl Carter* (Lawrence: University Press of Kansas, 1993), 8.

p. 28, "How do you explain . . ." Glad, *White House*, 126.

p. 29, "What they [the voters] want . . ." Ibid., 128.

p. 30, "The 46-year-old Governor . . ." Ibid., 141.

p. 31, "The time for racial discrimination is over . . ." Ibid.

CHAPTER FOUR: Carter and Ford

p. 40, "For the American Third Century . . ." Glad, *White House*, 230.

p. 41, "Surely the Lord . . ." Ibid., 280.

p. 44, "We've got something . . ." Ibid., 325.

p. 44, "We need your help . . . ." Ibid., 335.

p. 45, "I don't know how to compromise . . ." Ibid., 348.

p. 46, "If I ever tell a lie . . ." Ibid., 355.

p. 46, "He wavers, he wanders . . ." Ibid., 391.

p. 48, "In a spirit of individual . . ." Ibid., 469.

CHAPTER FIVE: Crisis of Spirit

p. 52, "We needed to correct . . ." Jimmy Carter, *Keeping Faith: Memoirs of a President* (Toronto: Bantam Books, 1982), 155.

p. 53, "You've got it all wrong . . ." Herbert D. Rosenbaum and Alexej Ugrinsky, eds. *Jimmy Carter: Foreign Policy and Post-Presidential Years* (Westport, Conn.: Greenwood Press, 1994), 161.

p. 58, "It was not pleasant . . ." Carter, *Keeping Faith*, 117.

p. 58, "It is a highly personal . . ." Glad, *White House*, 445.

p. 58, "crisis of spirit . . ." Kaufman, *James Earl Carter*, 145.

CHAPTER SIX: Campaigning Again

p. 63, "Human rights is the central . . ." Douglas Brinkley, *The Unfinished Presidency* (New York: Viking, 1998), 22.

p. 63, "Tapping this new spirit . . ." Glad, *White House*, 427.

p. 64, "This is the most serious . . ." Carter, *Keeping Faith*, 473

p. 64, "to lead the world . . ." Ibid., 472.

p. 64, "interrupting grain sales . . ." Ibid., 475.

p. 65, "None of these challenges . . ." Ibid., 525.

p. 66, "Are you better off . . ." Brinkley, *Unfinished Presidency*, 14.

p. 67, "I can't stand here . . ." Ibid., 1.

p. 69, "an altogether new . . ." Ibid., 44.

p. 70, "I'm not going to try . . ." Ibid., 48.

CHAPTER SEVEN: From President to World Citizen

p. 73, "a direct violation . . ." Brinkley, *Unfinished Presidency*, 109.

p. 73, "I've seen Carter sit . . ." Ibid., 112.

p. 76, "Star Wars is a scam." Ibid., 128.

p. 78, "Will we have planted . . ." Ibid., 177.

CHAPTER EIGHT: New Opportunities

p. 83, "There were, I would say . . ." Brinkley, *Unfinished Presidency*, 281.

p. 88, "As I have been . . ." Ibid., 279.

p. 88, "How can a great statesman . . ." Ibid., 279.

p. 89, "Come out and vote." Ibid., 281.

p. 90, "The government is taking . . ." Ibid., 285.

CHAPTER NINE: Promoting Democracy

p. 92, "We still helped to achieve . . ." Brinkley, *Unfinished Presidency*, 291.

p. 94, "Your greatest accomplishment . . ." Ibid., 307.

p. 96, "Yes, but you bring . . ." Ibid., 325.

p. 97, "In none of these cases . . ." Ibid., 337.

p. 99, "Bush acted as if . . ." Ibid., 414.

p. 99, "to prove that in at least one . . ." Bourne, *Character Portrait*, 500.

CHAPTER TEN: Committed and Tireless

p. 100, "I appreciate your offer . . ." Brinkley, *Unfinished Presidency*, 371.

p. 104, "My view was that . . ." Bourne, *Jimmy Carter*, 443.

p. 105, "Graves, graves, graves . . ." Ibid., 447.

p. 107, "We all owe you . . ." Ibid., 379.

CHAPTER ELEVEN: We Can Choose

p. 111, "[Carter] does more hard work . . ." Brinkley, *Unfinished Presidency*, 456.

p. 111, "Sometimes, I even have fun . . ." Ibid., 456.

p. 112, "We hope you will do . . ." Ibid., 456.

p. 112, "Guinea Worm, you better . . ." Ibid., 460.

p. 114, "Each of us can honor . . ." Ibid., 463.

p. 116, "for his decades of untiring effort . . ." The Nobel Peace Prize. http://www.nobel.no/eng_peace_2002.html.

p. 118, "I don't know . . ." Bill Adler, *The Wit and Wisdom of Jimmy Carter* (Secaucus, NJ: Citadel Press, 1977), 86.

p.118, "God gives us the capacity . . ." http://news.bbc.

Bibliography

Adler, Bill. *The Wit and Wisdom of Jimmy Carter*. Secaucus, NJ: Citadel Press, 1977.

Aburish, Saïd. *Arafat: From Defender to Dictator*. New York: Bloomsbury, 1998.

Bourne, Peter. *Jimmy Carter*. New York: A Lisa Drew Book, 1997.

Brinkley, Douglas. *The Unfinished Presidency*. New York: Viking, 1998.

Carter, Jimmy. *Keeping Faith: Memoirs of a President*. Toronto: Bantam Books, 1982.

Carter, Rosalynn. *First Lady from Plains*. Boston: Houghton Mifflin Company, 1984.

Glad, Betty. *Jimmy Carter: In Search of the Great White House*. New York: W.W. Norton & Co., 1980.

Hyatt, Richard. *The Carters of Plains*. Alabama: The Strode Publishers, Inc., 1977.

Kaufman, Burton I. *The Presidency of James Earl Carter*. Lawrence: University Press of Kansas, 1993.

Lasky, Victor. *Jimmy Carter: The Man & the Myth*. New York: Richard Marek Publishers, 1979.

Ledeen, Michael and William Lewis. *Debacle: The American*

Failure in Iran. New York: Alfred A. Knopf, 1981.

Mazlish, Bruce and Edwin Diamond. *Jimmy Carter: A Character Portrait.* New York: Simon and Schuster, 1979.

Miller, William Lee. *Yankee from Georgia: The Emergence of Jimmy Carter.* New York: New York Times Books, 1978.

Parmet, Herbert S. *George Bush: The Life of a Lone Star Yankee.* New York: A Lisa Drew Book, 1997.

Wooten, James. *Dasher: The Roots and the Rising of Jimmy Carter.* New York: Summit Books, 1978.

Websites

Biography of Rosalynn Carter: www.whitehouse.gov/history/firstladies/rc39.html

Carter Center: www.cartercenter.org

Carter Library and Museum: www.jimmycarterlibrary.org

Carter Timeline: www.pbs.org/wgbh/amex/carter/timeline.html

Character Above All: www.pbs.org/newshour/character/essays.carter.html

Jimmy Carter: www.american.president.org/KoTrain/courses/JC/JC_In_Brief.htm

Speeches by Jimmy Carter: www.tomu.edu/scom/pres/speeches/jccrisis.html

Jimmy Carter N.H.S. Education Program: http://www.jimmycarter.info/

Index